SPIRITUAL DISCIPLINES SERIES

SPIRITUAL JOURNALING

Recording Your Journey Toward God

A SMALL GROUP DISCUSSION GUIDE

RICHARD PEACE

NAVPRESS ●
BRINGING TRUTH TO LIFE
NavPress Publishing Group
P.O. Box 35001, Colorado Springs, Colorado 80935

Pilgrimage Publishing, Hamilton, Massachusetts

Cover illustration: Wood River Gallery

Printed in the United States of America

1 2 3 4 5 6 7 8 9 10 / 99 98 97 96 95

Contents

Acknowledgments

For some years now I have wanted to write a series of small group books on the theme of spiritual disciplines. For one thing, it seemed to me that learning about the spiritual disciplines with the help of others in a small group setting was the ideal approach, since the whole concept of spiritual disciplines is so alien to us in America. For another thing, I have found a renewed hunger in the American church, across all denominations, to recover the roots of our spiritual heritage. This hunger leads me to believe that the time is right for a series on the spiritual disciplines.

Lastly, I have found great personal help in my own spiritual life from the various disciplines. This is particularly true of journaling, to which I was introduced in the fall of 1975 when I attended my first Intensive Journal Workshop. This workshop was a profoundly important experience for me in that it taught me a method of personal and spiritual exploration that has become essential in my own spiritual pilgrimage. I owe a profound debt of gratitude to Dr. Ira Progoff, whose writings and workshops have significantly affected my life.

Progoff's ideas shine through at various places in this book. I have not slavishly followed his schema, however. Over the years I have adapted and expanded his materials. In particular, in teaching journaling to hundreds of theological students over the past fifteen years, I have tried to develop methods that incorporate the unique elements of Christian pilgrimage into the journaling process. I am grateful for all that I have learned from my students.

The Study Guide at a Glance

What's it all about?

This small group study guide is designed to teach you how to journal, and enable you to learn more about your spiritual pilgrimage through Bible study and sharing with others in your small group.

What will I learn?

- How to journal.
- Together with others in your small group, you will learn more about your own and others' spiritual pilgrimages.

How is the study guide put together?

Each of the seven chapters in this guide contains two 60–90 minute sessions:
1. *Learning to Journal:* material that describes some aspect of or concept in journaling, and an exercise designed to help you learn and experience it.
2. *Bible Study:* a Bible study designed to explore the life of someone in the Bible as a way of recalling and understanding incidents in our own pilgrimages, and recognizing God's activity and involvement in our lives.

At the end of each *Learning to Journal* session is a section called *Journal Readings*, which contains excerpts from a variety of journals. These are included to show different styles of personal reflection. In addition to the material in each of the seven chapters, there is an introductory chapter on the art of journaling, and an appendix of notes to small group leaders.

How will journaling benefit me?

- Journaling helps us pay attention to God. It is a way of hearing and responding to God.
- Journaling helps us understand our unfolding story. Knowing our story helps us to see what God has been doing in the past, is doing now, and is calling us to do in the future.

Is this course designed for church people only?

- No—anyone can join. All that is required is an interest in journaling and a spiritual openness to God. In fact, the small group would be a good experience for friends who are perhaps just beginning their own spiritual journey.
- The material in the study guide is written in "ordinary" language for the most part. When theological terms are used, they are explained.

How long will the study take?

- The material is best covered by meeting once a week for either seven or fourteen weeks. The group can do only the *Learning to Journal* exercises, only the *Bible Studies*, or all fourteen sessions.

- Other options include meeting every other week, doing all the sessions in two consecutive half-day Saturday seminars, or doing seven sessions at a weekend retreat.

What kind of small group commitment is involved?

In addition to attending all seven or fourteen sessions, each member should agree to abide by certain ground rules. These are discussed in the section entitled "Small Group Covenant" below.

What should I do to get ready for the first session?

Read *The Art of Journaling* (pp. 7–10). Here you will find a description of the journaling process and an overview of how the small group functions.

Is it necessary to do the journaling assignment?

- You will learn to journal by journaling, so the more time you can spend working in your journal during the week, the better.
- Some groups will begin each new session with a brief sharing time from the journal entries that were written during the week.
- Some weeks you may have no time to journal. You can still attend the group and learn the next method (which you can practice when you have time).

Small Group Covenant

Every small group should have a covenant (or contract) among members. Ground rules vary, but here are some typical ones:

- **Attendance:** I agree to be at the session each week unless a genuine emergency arises.

- **Participation:** I will enter enthusiastically into group discussion and sharing.

- **Confidentiality:** I will not share with anyone outside the group the stories of those in the group.

- **Honesty:** I will be forthright and truthful in what is said: if I do not feel I can share something, I will say "I pass" for that question.

- **Openness:** I will be candid with others in appropriate ways and allow others to share for themselves.

- **Respect:** I will not judge others, give advice, or criticize.

- **Care:** I will be open to the needs of others in appropriate ways.

Signed: _____

The Art of Journaling

Read this section before you begin the course.

We each have a story. Our stories tell who we are as they chart the unfolding of our lives and all of the factors that make each of us unique. Journaling is a means of helping us discern our stories, make sense of them, understand their significance, and connect them with God's story.

This course is about how to use a journal to assist your spiritual growth. The focus of the course is in three areas:
1. How to construct a journal;
2. How to use the journal to discern your personal story as a pilgrim; and
3. How to use the journal to track your spiritual development.

Constructing a Journal

A journal is a simple thing: blank pages in a notebook on which to record your musings. However, there are ways to construct a journal that make it a better tool for growth.

- Binding: While you can purchase bound books of blank pages with colorful covers, for this course you will need a journal which uses dividers. Also, you may find that loose-leaf binders give you more freedom to record "ordinary" and "mundane" thoughts as well as profound insights.

- Dividers: A journal is not just a diary in which you record each day's impressions. In a journal you record a variety of impressions, written from different vantage points and in different ways, with one section feeding into other sections. Thus to maximize the value of the journal, it helps to divide it into sections.

  The following divisions are suggested:
  Daily: in which you stay in touch with your life as it unfolds.
  History: reconstructing the contours of your past.
  Dialogue: engaging in a "conversation" form of journaling.[1]
  Pilgrimage: working on exercises to promote personal growth.
  Dreams: recording your nightly images.[1]
  Musings: recording your insights, thoughts, and reflections.
  Family: marking key events in the development of your family.
  Work: keeping notes and other materials related to your job.

- Size: There is no single or proper size for a journal. Larger formats permit more flexibility of use; smaller sizes are easier to carry. You must decide what size fits your life habits. You may have to experiment a little to find the size that is most comfortable and convenient for you.

- Paper: Whether you use lined or unlined paper is also a personal choice. I find that I need lines to guide my writing. Others prefer blank pages, especially if they do a lot of sketching. Of course, you can use both!

Using a Journal

The mechanics of journaling are important. Once in place, they provide the right context in which to do serious work. It is important to reflect on these issues and make choices.

- *When should I journal?* The short answer is "regularly." Just what "regularly" means will vary from person to person. Few people are able to journal on a daily basis—at least not for weeks or months at a time. The point is: use your journal to assist you; do not let it become a burden. However, when you are learning, try to journal at least three times a week for a while until the process becomes natural and easy for you.

  As to time of day, this will also vary from person to person. Some people need the freshness of morning when the mind is clear. Others will journal at the end of the day as a way to process the day's experiences. Still others journal at a point during their day when they have some quiet time.

- *Where should I journal?* You need a place where you can be alone and undisturbed. Journaling requires silence. You need inner space to reflect, pray, write, and read. Distractions make that difficult. Beyond this, people's needs vary. Find a setting that is comfortable and relaxing for you.

- *How long should I journal?* If possible, you should journal for as long as it takes to process what you are working with. In practice, people have limited time and must make do with whatever time is available. When you are learning to journal, try to set aside half-hour blocks of time, in order to get a feel for each journal exercise.

- *How should I journal?* Date each entry, including the year. Give a title to the entry so you will know where to file it. Then start writing. Don't worry about spelling, grammar, or complete sentences; just make it legible enough so that you can go back and read it at a later date.

  Privacy is important. Unless you are confident that you're writing for your eyes only, you won't be completely candid. And total honesty is essential. A journal is where you can express yourself without reservation or fear of consequences.

  While you may decide later to share portions of your journal with others, don't write with that thought in mind, or you might tailor what you write for their eyes.

- *What should I write?* The various exercises in this book will guide you as to what to write. Your attitude is important as you work on the exercises. An attitude of faith, of playfulness, of hope, and a willingness to know the way things really are will increase the value of journaling in your life.

  Journals are a tool for reflection. There is great power in putting thoughts on a page. Writing it down often sparks additional thoughts, insights, and concerns. You begin with a wisp of a thought and before you know it, you're on to something important in your life.

  Begin the process of journaling with prayer. Ask that the Holy Spirit guide you and guard you as you probe inner issues. Then trust God. This is the difference between a journal and a spiritual journal: conscious trust in God and dependence upon him.

Using a Journal to Discern Your Story

Journals are the first step in preparing a spiritual autobiography. It is by means of journal reflection that we get in touch with our past, recognize what is happening to us in the present, and develop a sense of where our future lies. As we do this, we begin to recognize the hand of God at work in our lives. The pieces of our past merge and become parts of a divine mosaic.

A spiritual autobiography, then, is the selection of incidents from a life that reveal the spiritual thread that wends its way through that life.[2]

Using a Journal to Grow Spiritually

Journaling is, itself, a spiritual discipline. It focuses mind and heart on the issues of growth with the aim of discerning what God is doing in one's life. By using a journal, we come in touch with our cutting edges of growth, those areas where questions exist or where there is need or longing. These are the areas in which the Holy Spirit often seems most active.

Journaling is also an aid to other spiritual disciplines. Writing down your insights is helpful in Bible study. Writing out your prayers helps you to communicate with God. Creating a poem that praises God is an act of worship. Journaling with others and sharing your work is a way to create Christian community.

The Power of Journaling in Groups

We need each other to learn the spiritual disciplines. It is hard to have a regular and consistent prayer life all on one's own. Worshiping God occurs in a corporate (as well as a private) setting. We need the insights of others as we study Scripture. Likewise, many people will learn to journal—and will be motivated to journal—by meeting with others who are also involved in this task.

Groups assist both the beginner and the experienced journaler. For the beginner, the rudiments of journaling are clarified as group members share how they experience the process. For the experienced journaler, a group will push him or her in new directions.

The journaling techniques you learn in each session will define the journaling process. At first, a new activity may feel somewhat strange. Keep working at it until it is comfortable and familiar to you. Eventually, you'll discover that some journal exercises work better for you than others. That's fine. There's nothing sacred about any particular exercise. They are simply tools designed to help you understand the meaning of your story.

The small group provides you the opportunity to share what you have learned about your pilgrimage with others who are also engaged in a spiritual pilgrimage. This is important, because journaling is never an end in itself; it is a means to spiritual growth.

Triggers

Writing in each section of your journal is not always a straightforward process. For example, you may begin at a place in your past, trying to get a feel for a troubling time. You write down the key people in your life at that time, and your sister's name triggers a thought of something you were supposed to do. The memory is troubling, beyond just the feeling of guilt over not keeping a commitment. So you shift over to the Present Period Log and work there for a while as you try to make sense of what is going on inside you.

Pay attention to triggers—those thoughts that spark memories, feelings, or ideas which sneak into your consciousness. These are not the issues you began reflecting on, but almost without warning, your mind moves to a new place. Be willing to give these "tangents" some space; they may prove to be quite important.

Or the tangent may just be that—a tangent. For example, it is not uncommon for a person to begin to pray, only to be reminded of a whole host of things he must do. This is a diversion from your real task. Over time, you will learn which tracks to follow and which to set aside so you can get back to the real issue.

Journal Bible Study

We can learn much from the story of others. We can learn how God acts in the lives of people, see how they respond in certain situations, and learn what to expect as we follow God. In the seven Bible studies in this series, we will explore the lives of various characters from Scripture, from the perspective of a journal each of them might have kept.

The Bible studies begin with careful observation of the text. We consider the background to the account. Then we ask: what do you suppose this person thought and felt in that situation? As we understand people in the Bible better, we understand our own stories better.

This Bible study also gives you another opportunity to journal. By examining the lives of various people, you will hear echoes from your own story. Use the Bible stories as a way to recall incidents in your life and as a way to evaluate the meaning of those incidents.

---

[1] Because inner dialogue, dreams, and other aspects of our inner world are of great interest in psychological and New Age circles, and are sometimes abused in Christian circles, some Christians suppose it is more biblical to focus on intellect than on imagination and dreams. While potential abuses abound and one should not make too much of dreams, inner dialogue, etc., biblical writers do repeatedly pay attention to these matters. I hope readers find in this guide a balanced approach to handling these topics, one that neither makes too much nor too little of them.

[2] In the second book of this series, *Spiritual Autobiography: Sharing Your Story*, the process of developing a spiritual autobiography will be discussed.

Chapter One

Using Journals Down Through History

"A journal is more than a diary;
it does not so much record our
days as record our spirits."

Journals have existed in many forms down through the ages. In all likeli-
hood, the earliest journals were oral, not written. A tribe would appoint
someone to "remember" its history, and on special occasions, this story-
teller would recount the events that made the tribe a unique people.

This was true of the Hebrews. They kept telling their story over and over
again and recorded it in what is today the Old Testament. Their stories
told of how God had sent their father Abraham on a long pilgrimage, how
Moses had led them out of Egypt through the Red Sea, how they entered
the Promised Land, and how they received a king. In these stories, the
Jews found their identity as a special people.

This was true for the earliest Christians as well. The accounts in the four
Gospels are simply written versions of oral stories that had been circulating
for years within the Christian community. The Gospels are, then, a journal of
the early church, recounting what Jesus taught, how he came to die for the
sins of the world, and how he changed the lives of the earliest believers.

We are most familiar with the journals that individuals keep. Some were
written by famous people—explorers like Richard Burton, missionaries like
Dr. David Livingstone, and theologians like Augustine. Some of these journals are elegant literary works. Sören Kierkegaard's journal has been called
one of the world's great masterpieces. Others offer great inspiration. The
journals of the famous mathematician and philosopher Blaise Pascal
(*Pensées*), or John Wesley (the founder of the Methodist church) have
moved readers to greater devotion and action.

But most journals are written by ordinary men and women. Never intended for anyone else to read, these journals are merely attempts to capture
the meaning of a person's life. Compared to the works of Augustine,
Pascal, and Wesley, they are not very profound or spiritually uplifting.
They may, in fact, border on being mundane. Yet, even these journals have
value for their authors: the journals allow them to "remember," and out of
"remembering," to see their unique journey of faith emerge.

For those who seek to follow Jesus, journals are a way to track their journey and to interact with Jesus as they continue on their way. Journals help
them to know themselves and God.

PART ONE/Learning to Journal

Session Overview

Effective journaling begins by noticing the larger context of our lives. In the first "Learning to Journal" session, you will begin to identify your Present Period.

Working with your Present Period gives you a way to notice the cutting edge of your spiritual life—the issues that confront you and which the Holy Spirit urges you to respond to. Working with your Present Period also helps you to understand the particular character of this phase of your life.

Telling Our Stories (15/20 minutes)

"Dear Diary…"

We may not have recognized them as such, but many of our efforts to preserve memories of the past were, in fact, forms of journaling. It is useful to examine the process of remembering.

1. Introduce yourself to the group:
   - What activity demands most of your attention during an average week?
   - What is one reason why you joined this group?

2. In which form(s) does your past exist?
   - ❏ in a diary
   - ❏ in family stories we still share at reunions
   - ❏ in old letters
   - ❏ in the memory of someone in my family
   - ❏ in a journal
   - ❏ in family records
   - ❏ in secrets shared with a friend
   - ❏ in my memory only
   - ❏ in no form that I know of

3. What experience of journaling (or of preserving something of your history) have you had as an adult? Of what use has this been to you?

The Journal Method (5 minutes)

The Present Period [1]

Life unfolds in phases. As you look back over time, you will realize that your life consists of a series of distinct periods, and that each period of time has its own character.

So, for example, I look back on my college years and realize that this period had a character quite unlike any time in my life before it or since. I had a particular set of friends: roommates, dormmates, classmates. I was engaged in a particular task: getting an education and acquiring the skills I would need in my career. I had certain authority figures that I listened to or reacted against: college professors, authors of the books I read, campus leaders. I lived a particular lifestyle: going to bed very late, eating in a college dining hall, structuring my time around the academic calendar. I reacted in certain ways to national issues in those days. I had particular spiritual and emotional concerns. Clearly college was unlike any other time of my life.

What is true of something like our college years is true throughout our lives. Life is a series of interconnecting periods of time, and each period has its own distinctive character. *So when we seek to understand who we are at any point in time, we must take into account the period in which we are living.* Our life at any point is bigger than the moment. Who we are, what we wrestle with, what we cherish, and what motivates us are all connected to the period we are living in.

Therefore, our journaling begins by seeking to understand the particular nature and character of the period of time in which we are now living: the Present Period.[2]

The Journal Exercise (15/30 minutes)

Preparation:
- Get out your journal. Find a comfortable spot in which to write. Date your journal. Entitle the entry: The Present Period.

- Do the focusing exercise. The small group leader will guide you in this process (see p. 85). Your aim at this point is to relax, focus on the topic, and ask the Holy Spirit to lead you as you journal.

Process:
There are two parts to this exercise: Period Image and Period Definition.

1. Period Image:
   With your eyes still closed, ask yourself this question:

   In what period of my life am I now living?

   Then simply notice what images, metaphors, feelings, and thoughts present themselves to you. Record these in your journal. However, keep your eyes partially closed, since you want to stay focused in this inward state. Do not evaluate what comes to you (you will assess this material at a later point); do not censor your thoughts; do not interpret these images. Instead, be alert not only to thoughts, but to physical sensations, images, and feelings.

2. Period Definition:
   Finding a Period Image gives you a feel for the time frame you are working with. Now the task is to define that period by identifying its distinguishing characteristics. In your journal, answer the following questions:

   • When did this period of life begin? Identify **the boundary** that separates this period from previous periods. This boundary may be a transition in your life (a new job, a new task, a new relationship), an event (an auto accident, the birth of a child), a new discovery (that you are called to a ministry), or a new decision (to prepare for a new career, to start work on a novel).

   • Who are the **key people** in your life during this period? What role does each play in your life? Which relationships are satisfying? Disappointing? Why?

   • What **distinguishing events** characterize this period of time? These may be personal or national events. Or, perhaps, the lack of anything new in your life is a distinguishing characteristic.

   • What are the **key concepts** that mark this time of life? What ideas are especially important to you now? What are you reading about? Thinking about? What interests you? What concepts are you wrestling with?

   • What are the **major responsibilities** that characterize this time period? In other words, how do you spend your time? What interests you most? Least? What is most creative about your life in this period? Most demanding?

   • What characterizes your **inner state** during this period? How would you describe your prayer life (active, inactive)? Reflective life? Emotional life?

   • What is your **physical state** during this period? Are you healthy? Not too well? What are your health challenges?

You will not have enough time to fully explore the Present Period. That will be your journaling task during the next week.

Journal Sharing (20/30 minutes)

When you finish journaling, discuss your findings with the group. Share at whatever level you are comfortable with.

1. Explore the process of journaling:
   - What was the easiest part of the process for you? Why?
   - What was the most difficult part of the process for you? Why?
   - What new thing did you learn about how to journal?

2. Share your insights from the journal experience:
   - What kinds of thoughts, impressions, experiences, etc., came to you during the Period Image exercise?
   - What is the boundary that marks the beginning of the Present Period for you?
   - What are some of your key insights into this period?
   - Describe the character of your Present Period: "These are the _____ years of my life."

3. Pray about this experience:
   - What single thing would you like the group to pray about?

Journaling Assignment (5 minutes)

You will learn how to journal by journaling. So it is important to journal during the week between small group meetings. During the next week:

- Expand your understanding of your Present Period. Do this by exploring within this period:

the key people	the key events
the key ideas	the key responsibilities
your inner state	your physical state

- Ask God to help you understand the key issues in your life during this Present Period, and the decisions you are being asked to make.

- Decide what you will share from your journal with your group at the next session. Each member will have two minutes to share at the start of the meeting.

Journal Readings

One of the better known contemporary journals is Henri J. M. Nouwen's *The Genesee Diary: Reports from a Trappist Monastery.* In it he describes his seven-month stay in a Trappist monastery where he wrestled with various questions about his relationship with God.

My desire to live for seven months in a Trappist Monastery, not as a guest but as a monk, did not develop overnight. It was the outcome of many years of restless searching. While teaching, lecturing, and writing about the importance of solitude, inner freedom, and peace of mind, I kept stumbling over my own compulsions and illusions. What was driving me from one book to another, one place to another, one project to another? What made me think and talk about "the reality of the Unseen" with the seriousness of one who had seen all that is real? What was turning my vocation to be a witness to God's love into a tiring job? These questions kept intruding themselves into my few unfilled moments and challenging me to face my restless self. Maybe I spoke more about God than with him. Maybe my writing about prayer kept me from a prayerful life. Maybe I was more concerned about the praise of men and women than the love of God. Maybe I was slowly becoming a prisoner of people's expectations instead of a man liberated by divine promises. Maybe . . . it was not all that clear, but I realized that I would only know by stepping back and allowing the hard questions to touch me even if they hurt . . . .

While realizing my growing need to step back, I knew that I could never do it alone. It seems that the crucial decisions and the great experiences of life require a guide. The way to "God alone" is seldom traveled alone.

About ten years ago, while on a long trip from Miami to Topeka, I stopped at the Trappist Abbey of Gethsemani in Kentucky, in the hope of finding someone with whom I could talk. When the guestmaster learned that I had studied psychology and was at the point of joining the faculty of a psychology department, he said with a happy twinkle in his eyes: "But we Trappists have a psychologist too! I will ask him to visit you." A little later Father John Eudes Bamberger walked into the guest room. Very soon I knew that I had met a rare and very convincing person. John Eudes listened to me with care and interest, but also with a deep conviction and a clear vision; he gave me much time and attention but did not allow me to waste a minute; he left me fully free to express my feelings and thoughts but did not hesitate to present his own; he offered me space to deliberate about choices and to make decisions but did not withhold his opinion that some choices and decisions were better than others; he let me find my own way but did not hide the map that showed the right direction. In our conversation, John Eudes emerged not only as a listener but also as a guide, not only as a counselor but also as a director. It did not take me long to realize that this was the man I had needed so badly.

Finally on June 1, 1974, after a lot of desk cleaning, I flew to Rochester, New York, to live as a Trappist monk for seven months, and on Pentecost, June 2, I started to write the notes that found their final form in this diary. [3]

PART TWO/Bible Study

Session Overview

Barnabas is a gentle saint of the first century, a man whose name keeps popping up in the story of the early church. He is a behind-the-scenes person who helps others (like Paul and Mark) to flourish.

Look at incidents in Barnabas' life and imagine what his journal might have contained. Then explore the parallels between his life and your life. Learn the meaning of your experience as you explore the meaning of his experience. Reflect on how you can become an encourager like Barnabas.

Telling Our Stories (15/20 minutes)

The Gentle Art of Encouragement

Joseph, the Levite from Cyprus, was known to the early church as Barnabas, which means "son of encouragement." Encouragement is a vital ingredient in the nurturing of relationships. Consider the role it has played in your life.

1. When you were a child, who encouraged you most? Describe that person.
   - ❐ my mother
   - ❐ a grandparent
   - ❐ a friend
   - ❐ a TV character (i.e., Mr. Rogers)
   - ❐ a character from a book
   - ❐ my father
   - ❐ a relative
   - ❐ a teacher
   - ❐ a sibling
   - ❐ other: _____

2. Whom do you encourage? How?
   - ❐ a child
   - ❐ a relative
   - ❐ a co-worker
   - ❐ a student
   - ❐ my spouse
   - ❐ an employee
   - ❐ a friend
   - ❐ other: _____

3. What do you need to learn about the art of encouragement?
   - ❐ to be sensitive to those who need encouragement
   - ❐ how to encourage without appearing to patronize
   - ❐ the nature of encouragement
   - ❐ to accept encouragement from others
   - ❐ how to be encouraging
   - ❐ to stay in the background and let others develop their skills
   - ❐ to speak the truth in love
   - ❐ other: _____

Exploring the Text (20/35 minutes)

Selections from the life of Barnabas

Read through each of the following passages from Acts, one at a time, and discuss the passage using the questions below. *Option:* Assign one passage to each group member and share answers after everyone has examined their passage.

1. Barnabas as a new believer: Acts 4:32–37
   - What do you learn from this passage about Barnabas' identity?
   - What might Barnabas have written in his journal about being a part of the early church in the days following the resurrection of Jesus?

2. Barnabas meets Paul: Acts 9:19–28
   - What role did Barnabas have in Paul's life when Paul came to Jerusalem as a new believer? Why was that an important role?
   - What might Barnabas have written in his journal about meeting Paul and helping him to be accepted in the early church?

3. Barnabas and the Antioch church: Acts 11:19–30
   - Why, do you suppose, did Barnabas bring Paul to Antioch with him?
   - What might Barnabas have written in his journal about his work in the Antioch church?

4. The first missionary journey: Acts 13:1–12
   - In how many different ways is the power of God evident in this passage?
   - What might Barnabas have written in his journal about the experience in Paphos with the sorcerer and false prophet?

5. In Lystra and Derbe: Acts 14:8–20
   - What might Barnabas have written in his journal about his experience in Lystra—being worshiped as the god Zeus one moment, and then seeing Paul attacked and left for dead a short time later?

6. Paul and Barnabas part company: Acts 15:36–41
   - Why did Paul and Barnabas split up?
   - What might Barnabas have written in his journal about this disagreement and separation from Paul—his long-time friend, advisee, and colleague?

Responding to the Text (20/30 minutes)

In your story:

1. Who are the well-known, talented, or public figures you have been involved with? What did your experience with them teach you?

2. When (if ever) have you stayed in the background and encouraged others to use their gifts? What did you learn? When (if ever) have you been out in front, using your gifts for the sake of God's kingdom?

3. What ministry situations have you been involved in? Discuss these.

4. Describe situations in which you have seen the power of God at work.

5. When (if ever) were you treated as someone very special or important? Describe the situation. How did you feel? When (if ever) were you dismissed or demeaned as someone unimportant? Describe the situation. How did you feel?

6. What was the most difficult separation you've ever experienced? What part was your fault? The other person's fault? Or was it a matter of people with different principles, values, or needs? How was the split repaired? If it hasn't been repaired, what will it take to make that happen?

Journal Assignment (5 minutes)

In your journal, continue to explore the story of Barnabas. Be attentive to parallels between his story and your story. In your journal, explore further the incidents in your life that you recalled during the small group discussion. Be alert to new insights about your past that emerge from examining your experiences in light of Scripture. Use the story of Barnabas as a way to recall incidents in your past. If you find it useful, write "the journal of Barnabas" as a way of understanding his story in Scripture.

Background Notes

- **Joseph the Levite:** A wealthy Jewish landowner from a priestly family on the island of Cyprus (in the eastern Mediterranean) who lived in Jerusalem during the days when the church was forming. He seemed to be held in high regard by the early church.
- **Paul's persecution:** Saul the Pharisee was one of the most feared men in the early church. He was determined to stamp out this new movement. In his zeal for what he thought was the truth, he was even willing to put Christians to death for heresy. He was there when Stephen was stoned to death (Acts 7:60). He persuaded the high priest to commission him to hunt down Christians in Damascus. As Paul put it in his speech at Jerusalem: "I persecuted the followers of this Way to their death, arresting both men and women and throwing them into prison" (Acts 22:4).
- **Paul's conversion:** It was while he was on his way to Damascus that Saul's life changed. Under the hot midday sun, he was struck down by an even greater light. A figure appeared to him and asked one simple question—a question that cut to the core of Saul's being and revealed to

him who he truly was: "Saul! Saul! Why do you persecute me?" Saul was baffled. He was not aware that he had been persecuting anyone. He was on a righteous mission, protecting God's truth. So he asked the logical question: "Who are you, Lord?" to which the voice replied: "I am Jesus of Nazareth, whom you are persecuting." With that insight, Saul was undone. He discovered himself to be a murderer and an enemy of God—not (as he thought) a zealous defender of God's truth. It was a devastating experience. But Jesus did not leave him in the dust. He told Saul to rise up and become his servant. Saul was given a mission: to be a witness for Jesus to his own people and to the Gentiles. The Pharisee Saul became the Apostle Paul.

- **Antioch:** The third most important city in the Roman Empire (behind Rome and Alexandria), found in modern-day Turkey. The first Gentile church developed a vigorous community here, and was the birthplace of the missionary movement (Acts 13). Paul's three missionary journeys originated from here.
- **the missionary journeys:** Paul made three extended missionary journeys, each time spreading the gospel further into the Roman world. (See Acts 13:1–14:28, 15:36–18:22, and 18:23–21:26.)
- **Zeus/Hermes:** Zeus was the ruler of the Olympian gods. Hermes (also known as Mercury) was the spokesman for the gods. There was an ancient legend that Zeus and Hermes once visited this region but were not recognized by anyone except an old couple. They were spared, but the rest of the people were killed in a flood. The townsfolk did not want to make this mistake again!
- **John Mark:** The young man who Paul and Barnabas took along on their first missionary journey was a relative of Barnabas. Mary, his mother, owned a large house in Jerusalem where the early church met. Why he left Paul and Barnabas at Perga (on the mainland of Asia Minor) is unknown. In any case, his inclusion in the second missionary journey became a point of contention between Paul and Barnabas, so they split up over the issue. Later on, however, Mark and Paul were reconciled (see Colossians 4:10). Mark also had a long association with Peter (see 1 Peter 5:13). Mark wrote the second Gospel.

---

[1] This concept, and others which follow, are taken from the seminal work of Dr. Ira Progoff (as described in his many books and in his Intensive Journal Workshops). I did my first Intensive Journal Workshop in the fall of 1975. It was a profoundly important experience in that it taught me a method of personal and spiritual exploration that I have used in my spiritual pilgrimage. I owe a profound debt of gratitude to Dr. Progoff.

[2] Ira Progoff calls this the Now Period.

[3] Henri J. M. Nouwen, *The Genesee Diary: Report from a Trappist Monastery* (Garden City, NY: Image Books, Doubleday, 1976), pp. 13–16.

Chapter Two

Using Journals to Cope with Our Present

"It takes so much time living my life that I have no time left for writing my life."

Journals help us to make sense of our lives. They cause us to notice what is happening to us—and in us—each day. They also allow us to respond to these realities.

So much happens every day. It has been estimated that the average American adult is exposed to over 16,000 separate sensory impressions each day. How do we notice all this, make sense out of it, or respond to it? Mostly, we don't notice and we don't respond. The result is that we drift through life rather than take hold of it.

But when we open a journal before us and record memories of the previous twenty-four hours, we begin to take charge of our lives. Journals help us:

- **Identify the significant events of each day.** Not all that happens to us is noteworthy. But in each day there are important ideas, feelings, decisions, actions, temptations, relationships, physical experiences, and spiritual events that shape us. Journals help us to notice all of this.
- **Respond to what we discover.** We do not have complete control over our lives. But we can make decisions about what we accept and what we reject; about what we will be like and what we won't be like. Journals help us to make decisions that promote growth.
- **Order our scattered lives.** For most of us, life is like an MTV video—all sorts of things are happening, flung at us in small doses in short time frames. What does it all mean? Who are we in the midst of all this input? Journals help us to make sense of what's happening to us.
- **Listen to God.** God is alive and present always. But we miss many signs of his presence if we don't pay attention. Journals help us to notice God.

Journals enable us to move from fog to clarity; to see our lives, feel our lives, live our lives. It is much easier to live in the past (through memories) or in the future (through fantasies) than to live in the present (through each moment). Journals make the present come alive for us.

To be a Christian pilgrim is to live in the present moment. It is a life with God: to seek him, to hear him, to respond to him, to worship and love him, and to obey him. Journals therefore become a vital tool for living in the present with God.

PART ONE/Learning to Journal

Session Overview

In this session, you will learn how to keep a Daily Log. You will also use this method to examine the past twenty-four hours of your life.

The Daily Log gives you a format to help you notice the presence of God each day, as well as to respond to what God is saying to you. Over time, this Log provides a record of the key events in your life which, when reviewed, gives you a reading on the character and direction of your life.

Telling Our Stories (15/20 minutes)

"Life is such a rush" [1]

For most of us, the problem is not finding things to do; it's finding time to do all the things we want—and need—to do.

1. Describe your typical weekday morning. What is the most hectic part of the morning for you? The most relaxed?

2. How do you cope with the pressure of your day?
   - ❐ exercise
   - ❐ sleep
   - ❐ pray
   - ❐ make jokes/laugh it off
   - ❐ explode
   - ❐ keep going
   - ❐ pretend there is no pressure
   - ❐ meditate
   - ❐ daydream
   - ❐ quit
   - ❐ think positively
   - ❐ I don't cope
   - ❐ what pressure?
   - ❐ other: _____

3. If time (and money) were no problem, which of the following would you most like to do? Why?
   - ❐ travel around the world
   - ❐ learn cordon bleu cooking
   - ❐ write a novel
   - ❐ paint seascapes of all the oceans
   - ❐ build a dream house
   - ❐ collect folk art
   - ❐ race Formula One cars
   - ❐ other: _____

The Journal Method (5 minutes)

The Daily Log

The most common use of a journal is to record and respond to the events of a day. This is the journal as diary. Here you write down the stuff of your life: the special things that happen—who you met, what you said, and how you felt; the challenges you faced, your emotional tone that day, and so on.

In your Daily Log you record not just what happened, but how you processed it. In fact, the "how" is generally more significant than the "what." For example, you meet a friend in the hall. You chat for a few minutes. Later, when you note the event in your Daily Log, you remember the tension you felt. You weren't especially happy to see your friend, but you didn't say anything. You ended the conversation quickly with an excuse about getting to a meeting. You remember the hurt look on her face. As you remember all of this, you ask yourself: "What's going on?" And so you begin to identify previously unacknowledged stress in an important relationship. The Daily Log allows you to process events from an *internal* perspective.

The Daily Log also allows you to process events from a *spiritual* perspective. After identifying a problem in your relationship, it is natural to pray about it right away. "Lord, what's going on here? Lori is a good friend. Help me to see the issue. Help me to be a good friend to her." Write out your prayer. And once you have prayed, listen. You asked God a question, so sit in silence. Be open to God. You may get some insight into the situation. Or you may remember a passage from Philippians, which you check out. Or you may move on to the next step in journaling, and keep the question you asked in the back of your mind.

The definition of a log is "a record of progress." In your Daily Log, you keep track of the unfolding of your life. When scanned as a whole, your log becomes a useful picture of where you have come from, where you are now, and where you seem to be heading.

You might also consider recording your dreams. Dreams can reveal what is going on inside you on an unconscious level. Recording them is simply extending the Daily Log into your sleeping hours. The point of dreams is not to discover some direct hotline to God so we don't have to use the normal means of Scripture, prayer, and meditation. While God can (and does) sometimes speak to his people in dreams, our intention at this point is to discover what our dreams say about us. By recording dreams in addition to the key elements of our day (activities, relationships, ideas, happenings, feelings, physical experiences, and spiritual events), we can review them to discern important themes and gain new insights. We will return to the topic of dreams in chapter 6.

The Journal Exercise (15/30 minutes)

Preparation:
- Get out your journal. Find a comfortable spot in which to journal. Date your journal. Entitle the entry: Daily Log.
- Do the focusing exercise, asking the Holy Spirit to lead you as you journal. The small group leader will guide you in this process (see p. 85).
- Begin journaling in silence for the time allotted.

Process:
Explore the previous twenty-four hours in your life:
- Make a time log. Recall how you spent the major blocks of time in the past twenty-four hours: What did you do yesterday evening? What was last night's sleep like? How did you spend your morning and afternoon? In other words, identify the character of the past day.
- Recall the details of each block of time. Identify in each time block:
    Major events: what you worked on, where you went, what you did, what you watched and listened to, and the other activities of the past twenty-four hours.
    Key relationships: whom you met, how you interacted, what you felt, what you said; the state of your various relationships.
    Important ideas: the ideas that caught your attention or troubled you, intrigued you, baffled you, amused you or challenged you. Note where you encountered these ideas and how they fit (or don't fit) into your worldview.
    External happenings in the world around you: the major news stories, the local events, incidents at work.
    Internal happenings in the world within you: dreams, sensations, intuitions, creative responses.
    Strongest feelings: positive (happiness, joy, excitement, contentment); negative (depression, bitterness, discouragement, disappointment, guilt); fear, anger, indifference, or hope.
    Notable physical experiences: how you felt; any exercise you had; headaches or other ailments; what you ate and drank; the sexual side of your life.
    Spiritual events: recall your experience in prayer, Bible study, worship and other spiritual disciplines; note the sense of God's presence.
    Conclusions reached: your assessment of the day, the choices you made, your responses; questions you are left with.

The aim of this exercise is *not* to write every detail of the past twenty-four hours. Rather, the aim is to pinpoint the key elements of the past day—whether activities, relationships, ideas, happenings, dreams, feelings, physical experiences, or spiritual events. Use the checklist above as a way of finding where the focus of your day was. In most cases, one or two categories will dominate your day. Explore these. In particular, notice the conclusions you reached—some of which you will not have noticed. While you are journaling, you may also make some new decisions. In other words, notice and interact with your previous day.

Journal Sharing (20/30 minutes)

When you finish journaling, discuss your findings with the group.

1. Explore the process of journaling:
   - What was the easiest part of the process for you? Why?
   - What was the most difficult part of the process for you? Why?
   - What new thing did you learn about how to journal?

2. Share your insights from the journal experience:
   - What did you discover about the structure of your day when you made the time log?
   - As you scanned the past twenty-four hours with respect to the various categories, which one(s) dominated your day? How? Why?
   - What was your key insight into the past twenty-four hours?
   - What conclusions did you reach about your day?

3. Pray about this experience:
   - What single thing would you like the group to pray about?

Journaling Assignment (5 minutes)

During the next week:

- Read over all of the material in the chapter, including the excerpt from *The Journals of Jim Elliot.*

- Practice working with your Daily Log. Do at least three daily entries during the week. Explore your days by examining:

major events	internal happenings
key relationships	strongest feelings
important ideas	notable physical experiences
external happenings	spiritual events

- Ask God to help you understand the key issues in your life. What issues are you wrestling with now?

- Discern what new insights you have into your unfolding story.

- Decide what you want to share with your group during the next session from your Daily Log. Remember that you will have only two minutes. Share things that will help the group know you—perhaps exciting or new discoveries. Be willing to be appropriately open with the group in what you share.

Journal Readings

The Journals of Jim Elliot

Jim Elliot was one of five young missionaries murdered by the Auca Indians in Ecuador in 1956. His journal was later edited (but not abridged) by his widow, Elisabeth Elliot. This is the kind of journal most men and women write. It was never intended to be published. It records the ordinary struggles and victories of an honest and devout young man who sought to know and serve God. This excerpt was written in Ecuador sometime between 1952 and 1955.

June 8
Heard brother Crisman (fifty years in Ecuador) at the Second Church in the morning. Lord, let me learn to speak Spanish in fifty years—seems as if no one really gets past the beginner's stage in pronunciation of all the gringos I've met. And none hit the national's genius of language. Give of the gift of tongues! Let me speak to them as they ought to be spoken to, so they do not have to hide their real reaction with polite praise. Glad to be in a national home—at least to hear it spoken as a living-thought medium—not merely as English translation.

Mist and rain under the slim, sharp silhouetted eucalyptus with her [his future wife, Betty Elliot], then the mud-arch doorway out of the wet. Talked of her relation with Dorothy and some of the problems. Lord, I'm asking for the very best for them; let them learn friendship in the full sense. Betty doesn't seem to really want intimacy with D. J.—something my personality will never understand. Let me deal wisely here, Lord, if I should counsel or suggest. Felt very much outside the situation as far as really being able to analyze it, yet somehow so close to it with my feelings for Betty—wanting the very happiest for her, and sensing a certain responsibility to achieve it for her. She admits a problem and confesses that she doesn't know the way through it, but I fear she doesn't really want it solved badly enough. Her natural reserve is strong; she only gets intimate with those who "happen to fit"—or, as she says, "with those friendships that are outright gifts from God." Although she recognizes that some friendships must be made, I think she is not willing to expend the effort to make one with D. J.—mainly because she doesn't really believe that they are a pair, she doesn't think D. will really be capable of being "made" a comrade.

I agree. D. doesn't look like the right kind of stuff. But, oh, how I want to see Betty happy these waiting years without each other, and an intimate with whom she could share things would be such a boon. Still, she says as I said when D. was en route to New York, they have nothing in common. Outwardly, no. Betty is poetic, fond of nature, penetrating. Dorothy seems superficial, childish, ingenuous beside her. But, Father, they have Christ in common, and I want You to teach them how to share Him. I can't expect D. to be for Betty what Pete has been for me, but at least she can be some sort of outlet to confer with, some sort of balance to stabilize all Betty's inwardness. Sure seems like a good problem, Lord. I am waiting to see You work it out.[2]

PART TWO/Bible Study

Session Overview

Paul is one of the great figures in the New Testament. He founded the church in Europe, making him our spiritual forebear. Paul burned with a relentless zeal that drove him on three missionary journeys, during which he founded dozens of churches. His fiery personality caused him to oppose anyone who would corrupt or dilute the gospel of Christ. Yet he was also soft and tender toward others, longing for them to know his Lord. It is hardly possible in six passages to capture the essence of this man, but you will begin to understand Paul as you watch him in his pilgrimage from being a zealous persecutor of the church to being its zealous champion.

Look at incidents in the life of Paul and consider what his journal might have contained, if he had kept one. Then explore the parallels between his life and your life. Learn the meaning of your experience as you explore the meaning of his experience. Reflect on how you can become as zealous for the gospel as Paul was.

Telling Our Stories (15/20 minutes)

Zeal

If he was anything, Paul was zealous. He was zealous as a young man—he became a Pharisee and reached the pinnacle of first-century Jewish spirituality. He was equally zealous as a founder and defender of the church.

1. From the list below, pick one thing which you are (or might be) enthusiastic about. Explain.

❏ animals	❏ reading
❏ relaxing	❏ the arts
❏ crafts	❏ music
❏ sports	❏ gardening
❏ cooking	❏ conversation
❏ film	❏ other: _____

2. What do you think is the one key sign of a true enthusiast? Explain.

❏ time spent	❏ conversational focus
❏ energy invested	❏ aspirations concerning
❏ preoccupation with	❏ love of
❏ creativity given	❏ other: _____

3. What's the best thing about having a passion? What's the worst thing?

Exploring the Text (20/35 minutes)

Selections from the life of Paul

Read through each of the following passages, and discuss them using the questions below. (See the option on p. 18.)

1. Saul the persecutor: Acts 7:51–8:3
   - Why were the Jews (including Saul) so angry at the early church?
   - What might Saul have written in his journal about the death of Stephen and his own role as a persecutor of the church?

2. Paul and the Judaizers: Acts 15:1–21
   - Who were the opposing groups, and what was the issue that divided them? How was the issue resolved?
   - What might Paul, the ex-Pharisee, have written in his journal about this debate and his views on it?

3. Paul in Athens: Acts 17:16–34
   - What was first-century Athens like?
   - What was the essence of Paul's message?
   - How might Paul have described his day in Athens when he wrote in his journal that evening?

4. Paul before Agrippa: Acts 25:23–26:32
   - Describe the nature of Paul's argument to King Agrippa.
   - In his journal, how might Paul have described his conversion? His experience with King Agrippa?

5. Paul's shipwreck: Acts 27:27–28:10
   - Describe the various ways in which the power of God worked through Paul in this incident.
   - In his journal, how might Paul have described the experience of God's power in foretelling the future or healing a person?

6. Paul's vision: 2 Corinthians 12:1–10
   - Describe Paul's mystical experience.
   - How did Paul deal with his suffering?
   - In his journal, how might Paul have described what it was like to know both visions and suffering?

Responding to the Text (20/30 minutes)

In your story:

1. Have you been involved in a crusade for or against an issue? Describe your experience. What were the positive and negative aspects of that experience? How do you know when you are "on the side of angels"?

2. Have you ever gone through a legalistic period in your life when rules and regulations were very important? Describe the experience. What are some of the basic principles by which you govern your life and behavior? Where are you now when it comes to "following the spirit rather than the letter of the law"?

3. When (if ever) have you investigated the claims of Christianity? Describe the process. How do you deal with the question of the truth of Christianity? What convinces you of the fact of Jesus' resurrection?

4. In what ways was your conversion similar to (or different from) Paul's? What other experiences have you had that are like Paul's encounter with Jesus on the Damascus Road?

5. In what ways have you experienced the power of God in healing, guidance, prophecy, or prayer? Describe the most amazing case of healing by faith that you know of. Is God's power still active in our world today in the same way it was in the first century? Discuss the reasons for your response to this question.

6. What mystical experiences have you had, if any? Describe their impact on your life. What has been your experience of suffering? How has suffering been a means of grace for you?

Journal Assignment (5 minutes)

In your journal, continue to explore the story of Paul. Be attentive to the parallels between his story and your story. In your journal, explore further the incidents in your life that you recalled during the small group discussion. Be alert to new insights into your past that emerge from examining your experiences in light of Scripture. Use the story of Paul as a way to recall other incidents in your past. If you find it useful, write "the journal of Paul" as a way of understanding his story in Scripture.

Background Notes

- **Stephen:** One of the leaders of the church in Jerusalem who was stoned to death following his speech to the Sanhedrin (Acts 7:1–53). He interpreted Jewish history in a way that they considered to be blasphemous; thus Stephen became the first Christian martyr.
- **Saul:** In New Testament times, individuals had various names. Paul was also known as Saul. At his conversion, Jesus gave Saul his new name.
- **Judaizers:** A group of Jewish Christians in the early church who argued that Gentiles had to become Jews first before they could become Christians. Paul realized that this was antithetical to Jesus' message of grace. Salvation was a gift from God, not a matter of ethnicity. So Paul

strenuously opposed the Judaizers. He understood that if they gained a foothold in the early church, it would inhibit the gospel from spreading to the Gentile world and would distort the message of Jesus.

- **circumcision:** Circumcision was the test of compliance to Jewish law.
- **idols, immorality, meat, blood:** These prohibitions relate to weaknesses in the Gentile community that might affect their lifestyle as Christians. They might be tempted to return to idolatry or sexual sin (which was tolerated in the Gentile community), or alienate tolerant Jews.
- **Athens:** The site of a leading university and the home of philosophy.
- **an unknown god:** Paul argues that God can be known; that God is personal (not a dead idol made of stone); and that it is through Jesus—who was resurrected from the dead—that God can be known.
- **Festus, Agrippa, Bernice:** Festus was the Roman governor of Judea; Herod Agrippa II ruled over territory in the northern regions of Palestine; Bernice was his sister.
- **resurrection:** The issue that the Jews cannot resolve is the resurrection of Jesus. If he had been raised from the dead (as Paul argued), then Jesus was the Messiah they were expecting. Paul becomes convinced of the resurrection when he meets the living Jesus on the road to Damascus.
- **miracles:** The early church experienced the power of God in many ways: by healing that occurred through the laying on of hands and praying, through prophesies that accurately predicted the future, and even by seeing the dead raised.
- **boasting:** The false prophets who plagued the Corinthian church force Paul to "boast" about his accomplishments (as they do). He finds this very distasteful, but apparently this is the only way to get the Corinthians to listen.
- **visions and revelations:** The false prophets boasted that their teaching came directly from God, so Paul talked about his ecstatic experiences. He mentions them, however, in the context of his suffering, not as a claim to fame. The exact nature of his experience cannot be determined, except to describe it as an amazing mystical experience.
- **a thorn in the flesh:** No one knows what Paul's problem was. Speculation has ranged from a physical malady (such as ophthalmia, epilepsy, or malaria) to sexual temptation, to the intense and unrelenting opposition from his enemies. Whatever the problem was, Paul learned to cope with it and make it a source of grace from God.

---

[1] From now on you have a choice of how you begin each session. You can use the printed exercise, or you can begin by sharing insights from each person's journaling during the previous week. If you decide to share insights from journaling, go around the circle and give each person a chance to share briefly.

[2] *The Journals of Jim Elliot*, ed. by Elisabeth Elliot (Old Tappan, NJ: Fleming H. Revell Co.,1978), pp. 393–394.

Chapter Three

Using Journals to Recover Our Past

- *"There are vivid memories to be sure; but*
- *there are also dark gaps. It is in those gaps*
I must look to know who I am."

John Calvin begins his influential work, *Institutes of the Christian Religion*, with the statement that true wisdom has two parts: knowledge of God and knowledge of self. As Christians, we turn to the Bible in our search to know God. But what about the search to know ourselves? This is where journals come in. They facilitate not only a daily awareness of who we are becoming, but they also help us probe the past to know who we've been.

This is a vital task if you are to discern clearly the main lines in the story of your spiritual pilgrimage. You cannot really know who you are now—much less who you are to become—unless you know who you were as a child, as a teenager, as a young adult, as a newlywed, and so on.

But how do we get a handle on the past? It is often so murky. We seem to have forgotten so much. And what we do remember is not always reliable. In his journal workshops, Ira Progoff suggests that we treat our past not as a single and undifferentiated whole, but as a series of interconnected periods. Each period has its own character; each period yields its own data about who we were at a particular point in time.

Of course, it would have been helpful if we had kept detailed journals from the time we could write, but few of us have done that. In any case, all that they would show is how we understood ourselves at that time. This, of course, would not have been fully accurate. The way we now assess our turbulent adolescent years is quite different from what we understood when we went through them. Progoff argues that what we need to know is our history from an internal point of view—not just the "facts," but what the people, events, ideas, and emotions meant to us in each period of time.

For some of us, examining the past may be a difficult thing to do. There may be painful memories or broken relationships we'd rather leave alone. But even though it may be hard to probe the pain of the past, it's important to do so. In fact, the present can be the best time to examine these things—as time passes, the pain loses some of its sting, and we have matured (so we are able to explore and understand what happened).

By reviewing our past, we also begin to recognize the footprints of God in our life. They weren't always clear at the time. But in retrospect, we can see patterns. We come to understand how God was at work, shaping and preparing us for unique opportunities of ministry and service. And so we understand our story from a spiritual—as well as a historical—point of view.

PART ONE/Learning to Journal

Session Overview

A hinge is a turning point, when life moves from one direction to another. Generally, hinge events are not very dramatic—for example, moving fifty miles to start a new job. But in retrospect, we see that life changed because of that move.

In this session, you will identify a series of hinge-points in your life and see how they mark the periods of your life. Identifying these periods will help you to discover your story and to see the various ways in which God has been at work in the past.

Telling Our Stories (15/20 minutes)

Memories

The ability to remember is a great gift, because in this way we can relive the high points in our lives.

1. Which period of time was the most fun for you? Which was the most challenging? Put a "+" on the line for the fun time, and a "−" for the challenging. Explain your choices.
   ___ grade school   ___ high school
   ___ college   ___ my twenties
   ___ my thirties   ___ mid-life
   ___ my fifties   ___ retirement

2. Pick one of the categories below and describe a great experience or event connected to it:
   ❑ special vacations   ❑ fun accomplishments
   ❑ historic events   ❑ unforgettable meals
   ❑ great gatherings   ❑ meaningful milestones
   ❑ memorable moments   ❑ aesthetic experiences

3. If you could arrange a memorable event for you and your family, what would you do?

The Journal Method (5 minutes)

Hinges

The first step in examining the past is to divide your life into a series of time periods that make sense to you. In this exercise, what you are looking for are transitional events or *hinges:* actions, ideas, experiences, or encounters that move your life in a new direction. For example, you leave home for the first time at eighteen to attend a college 600 miles away: *going to college* marks a shift in your life and so qualifies as a hinge event. Or you have an auto accident in which you break both legs: *the accident* launches a new phase in life in which you learn about dependence and pain. *Marriage* almost always qualifies as a transitional event, as does *conversion* or *induction into the armed services.*

There are various *types* of events that often turn out to be hinge incidents:
* A move from one place to another: away from your childhood home; to a new city, state, or country; to a new job; to a new challenge.
* A new person comes into your life: a spouse, a child, a mentor, a friend, an enemy, a boss, an employee, a relative, a pastor.
* A new phase of education: grade school, middle school, high school, college, graduate school, seminary, professional seminars.
* A new commitment: marriage, birth of a child, joining a church, beginning a business, taking out a mortgage.
* A traumatic incident: death of a loved one, arrest, an accident or illness, unexpected success or failure, loss of a job.
* A religious experience: conversion, an answer to prayer, a mystical encounter, a retreat, a worship experience, a small group.
* A national event: a war, a recession, new legislation, death of a leader or hero, a shift in national perception.
* A new idea: about truth, reality, or morality; encounter with a book, film, or a piece of music; experiencing a new group, culture, or discipline.
* A creative venture: beginning to write poetry, to play the saxophone, or to read biographies; starting a journal or a potter's shop; taking up photography or exploring back roads.

When we have defined these hinges, we have divided our lives into a series of periods. The challenge, then, is to begin to understand the character of the time periods between hinge events. What did we become in that period, and how has it made us who we are today? In particular, we need to recall for each period:

* the key people
* the activities or responsibilities that demanded our time and energy
* the important ideas
* the nature of inner life: the dreams, images, longings, and emotions
* the nature of our health then: exercise, sport, diet, and illness
* the creative impulses that shaped us
* the external events that shaped us: events on the national, state, and local scene and their impact on us; the nature of our personal environment

There is no single or correct way to divide your life. In fact, if you did this exercise again in a few years, your hinges would probably be different. You would find some events on both lists, but other events would emerge as crucial. It all depends on your point of view as you look back on your life.

The Journal Exercise (15/30 minutes)

Preparation:
- Get out your journal. Find a comfortable spot in which to journal. Date your journal. Entitle the entry: Hinges. File this in the History section of your journal.
- Go over the directions below that describe the journaling exercise.
- Do the focusing exercise, asking God the Holy Spirit to lead you as you journal.
- Begin journaling, in silence, for the time allotted.

Process:
There are three parts to this exercise.

1. Hinges:
   With your eyes still closed, ask yourself this question:

   What are the hinge events in my life?

   Start your list with the entry "Birth" and then write down the eight to twelve events of your life (these numbers are important) that spontaneously present themselves to you. Don't think too hard about finding events. Just relax and in an attitude of prayer, open yourself to the ideas that come to you. At this point, do not evaluate what you write (you will work with this material at a later point in the exercise); do not censor your thoughts; do not interpret these images; instead, just be alert to them.

2. Chronology:
   Now go back over your list of hinge events and put them in chronological order, adding any descriptive phrases that occur to you about the time period that follows the hinge event.

3. Description:
   Begin working with one of these time periods. It doesn't matter which one (though you will probably be drawn to one of the hinge events and the period that follows). Using the categories in the Present Period exercise (chapter 2), describe the period by writing: "It was a time when . . ." and then describe the key people, distinguishing events, key concepts, external events, major responsibilities, your inner state, your physical state, and any spiritual events. (For a fuller description of each of these categories, consult the Journal Exercise section in chapters 1 and 2.) You will not have enough time to explore fully the period you have chosen. That will be your journaling task this week. In fact, it will be your task over the next months to explore each period in this way, as you seek to understand your story and see God's hand in it.

Journal Sharing (20/30 minutes)

When you finish journaling, discuss your findings with the group.

1. Explore the process of journaling:
   - What was the easiest part of the process for you? Why?
   - What was the most difficult part of the process for you? Why?
   - What new thing did you learn about how to journal?

2. Share your insights from the journal experience:
   - What are some of the hinge events in your life? Which events on this list surprised you? Which events were obvious?
   - Which time period stands out as special or significant for you now as you explore your history? Explain.
   - What new insights did you come to about your past?
   - In what ways did this exercise challenge you?

3. Pray about this experience:
   - What single thing would you like the group to pray about?

Journaling Assignment (5 minutes)

During the next week:

- Read over all of the material in the chapter, including the excerpt from *The Journal of John Wesley.*

- Pick a particular time period to explore. Explore it by using the categories suggested in the exercise:

major events	internal happenings
key relationships	strongest feelings
important ideas	notable physical experiences
external happenings	spiritual events

- Ask God to help you understand the key issues in your life during this period. In what ways was God present in your life then?

- What new insights do you have into your unfolding story? What is the shape and character of your spiritual pilgrimage during this period?

- Decide what you want to share with your group during the next session from your period exploration. Remember that you will have only two minutes. Share things that will help the group know you. Share exciting or new discoveries for you. Be willing to be appropriately open with the group in what you share.

Journal Readings

Wesley wrote two journals. The one he intended to publish (*The Journal of John Wesley*); the other, which he called his diary, was private. Wesley drew from his private diary in the preparation of his public journal. Wesley's journal ranged far and wide in the subjects it covered. Still, at its heart, it is a vivid description of the work of God in the lives of various men and women. Wesley describes here some critical events for him: the fear that his beloved brother was dying, coupled with a new understanding of the nature of faith that transformed his ministry:

> *Tues. 28. I saw my mother once more. The next day I prepared for my journey to my brother at Tiverton. But on Thursday morning, March 2d, a message that my brother Charles was dying at Oxford, obliged me to set out for that place immediately. Calling at an odd house [an out-of-the-way house] in the afternoon, I found several persons there who seemed well-wishers to religion to whom I spake plainly; as I did in the evening, both to the servants and strangers at my inn.*
>
> *With regard to my own behaviour, I now renewed and wrote down my former resolutions.*
>
> *1. To use absolute openness and unreserve, with all I should converse with.*
>
> *2. To labour after continual seriousness, not willingly indulging myself in any the least levity of behaviour, or in laughter—no, not for a moment.*
>
> *3. To speak no word which does not tend to the glory of God; in particular, not to talk of worldly things. Others may, nay, must. But what is that to thee? And,*
>
> *4. To take no pleasure which does not tend to the glory of God; thanking God every moment for all I do take, and therefore rejecting every sort and degree of it, which I feel I cannot so thank him in and for.*
>
> *Sat. 4. I found my brother at Oxford, recovering from his pleurisy; and with him Peter Böhler; by whom (in the hand of the great God) I was, on Sunday, the 5th, clearly convinced of unbelief, of the want of that faith whereby alone we are saved.*
>
> *Immediately it struck into my mind, "Leave off preaching. How can you preach to others, who have not faith yourself?" I asked Böhler, whether he thought I should leave it off or not. He said, "Preach faith till you have it; and then, because you have it, you will preach faith."*
>
> *Accordingly, Monday, 6, I began preaching this new doctrine, though my soul started back from the work. The first person to whom I offered salvation by faith alone, was a prisoner under sentence of death. His name was Clifford. Peter Böhler had many times desired me to speak to him before. But I could not prevail on myself so to do; being still (as I had been many years) a zealous assertor of the impossibility of a death-bed repentance . . . .* [1]

PART TWO/Bible Study

Session Overview

In this Bible study our focus is on Ruth, a woman from the Old Testament. Ruth lived through a very difficult time (the death of her husband). Rather than take the easy route and return to her own family and tribe, she chose to stay with Naomi, her mother-in-law, even though this meant going into a foreign country where her future was dubious. Her faithfulness, care, loyalty, and faith are rewarded in quite remarkable ways. She becomes the great-grandmother of David and hence, an ancestor of Jesus.

Look at incidents in the life of Ruth and reflect on what her journal might have contained.

Telling Our Stories (15/20 minutes)

Finding a Spouse

Seeking and/or finding a spouse is a deeply important part of the life story of many people. The usual tale is a mix of excitement, trauma, wonder, agony, and fulfillment. (Please note that the questions below are directed, for the most part, to those who are married. Of course, not everyone is married! Adapt the questions to your own circumstance.)

1. Describe how you met your spouse (or your former spouse).

2. What was the best part of your courtship (or courtship in general)? The worst part?

3. Which question would you like to ask the opposite sex about courtship? Let the opposite sex in your group reply!

Exploring the Text (20/35 minutes)

Selections from the life of Ruth

Read through each of the following passages from the Book of Ruth, and discuss them using the questions below. (See the option on p. 18.)

1. Naomi and Ruth: Ruth 1:1–14
   - How had Naomi come to Moab in the first place, and why did she decide to return to Bethlehem?
   - Why does Naomi urge her daughters-in-law to remain in Moab?
   - How might Naomi have described in her journal the time when she lived in Moab?

2. Ruth comes to Bethlehem: Ruth 1:15–22
   - Why does Ruth decide to accompany her mother-in-law to this foreign land?
   - In her journal, how might Naomi have described what she felt like when she returned to Bethlehem? What would she have written about Ruth?

3. Ruth meets Boaz: Ruth 2:1–12
   - Describe the circumstances under which Ruth and Boaz meet and how each responds.
   - What does this passage show us about the character of Boaz? The character of Ruth?
   - In her journal, what might Ruth have written about living in a foreign land, as a widow with no income?

4. Ruth requests Marriage: Ruth 3:1–13
   - In this rather unusual situation (to our Western eyes) what was the role of Naomi? The role of Ruth? The role of Boaz?
   - What might Ruth have written about that night with Boaz?

5. Boaz marries Ruth: Ruth 4:1–12
   - Describe the events that lead to the marriage of Boaz and Ruth.
   - How do you respond to these ancient marriage customs?
   - What might Ruth have written about her upcoming marriage to Boaz?

6. Ruth bears a child: Ruth 4:13–22
   - What is the outcome of Naomi's story? Of Ruth's story? Of the story of Israel?
   - How might Ruth have summed up her life in her journal?

Responding to the Text (20/30 minutes)

In your story:

1. What was the most difficult period in your life? Why? In what ways was the hand of God present during that difficult time?

2. Is there anything in your life that parallels the experience of Ruth (in committing herself to Naomi and accompanying her on a journey into the unknown)? Describe it and the outcome in your life.

3. Recall instances when you've been unexpectedly blessed by the kindness of strangers, or when you had what looked like a stroke of good luck. In what ways was God present in that experience?

4. How did you come to be engaged (if you have been engaged)? On what basis do we choose the person we intend to spend our lives with?

5. Describe your marriage (if you are married). How does it differ from Ruth's experience? In what ways is it similar?

6. In what ways is your story intertwined with the stories of others? How have your actions affected the story of your family?

Journal Assignment (5 minutes)

In your journal, continue to explore the story of Ruth. Read through the book again. Examine the passages you did not cover in the small group. Be attentive to the parallels between her story and your story. In your journal, explore further the incidents in your life that you recalled during the small group discussion. Be alert to new insights about your past as they emerge by examining your experiences in light of Scripture. Use the story of Ruth as a way to recall other incidents in your past. If you find it useful, write "the journal of Ruth" as a way of understanding her story in Scripture.

Background Notes

- **Moab:** A region on the east side of the Dead Sea. There was great hostility between those from Judah (one of the tribes of Israel located on the other side of the Dead Sea) and the Moabites. The source of this hostility was the Israelite invasion of the region. Bethlehem was on the west side of the Dead Sea, fifty miles or so from Moab.
- **Naomi's husband died:** It was almost impossible for a widow without sons to survive on her own. When a woman lost her husband, she lost her place in society and had to depend on others.
- **Ruth:** Ruth, who was a Moabite (not an Israelite), is the great-grandmother of King David and an ancestress of Jesus (see Matthew 1:1,5).
- **full/empty:** This is the key motif in this book. Naomi is stripped of everything, but due to the faithfulness of Ruth and the provision of God, she becomes full again.
- **harvest:** Grain was harvested in April and May. This involved the cutting of grain with a hand sickle, binding it into sheaves, threshing it (removing the grain from the stalk), and winnowing (tossing the grain into the air to separate the grain from the chaff).
- **leftover grain:** Old Testament law instructed farmers to leave behind the grain the harvesters missed and to allow the poor and the widowed to gather this for themselves.
- **tonight he will be winnowing:** During harvest, it was common for landowners to sleep near their grain in order to protect it from thieves.
- **wash and perfume yourself:** These are preparations that a bride would make for her wedding day.
- **eating and drinking:** Harvest time was a time of celebration.
- **uncover his feet and lie down:** This situation in the threshing room strikes the modern reader as aggressive (on Naomi's part in her instructions to Ruth), and sexually charged. In fact, it was more innocent than it appears. Ruth's actions (guided by Naomi) were a request for marriage, appealing to Boaz in his role as the kinsman-redeemer. In this case, Boaz had already displayed his concern for (and interest in) Ruth so that Naomi is aware that he might want to marry her. In this narrative, Ruth's character is never in doubt (see 3:11).
- **kinsman-redeemer:** The closest male relative had the responsibility to marry a widow. Boaz must give the kinsman-redeemer the opportunity to marry Ruth if he chooses.
- **town gate:** This is where business was conducted in ancient villages.
- **you acquire the dead man's widow:** In order to keep alive the name of Mahlon (Ruth's dead husband), her firstborn son would bear his name and inherit the land. The unnamed kinsman perhaps fears that should he have a son by Ruth (who is his only heir), all of his land would go to the family of Elimelech (Naomi's dead husband).

---

[1] *The Journal of John Wesley: A Selection by John Wesley*, edit. by Elisabeth Jay (Oxford: Oxford University Press, 1987), pp. 27–28.

Chapter Four

Using Journals to Interact with Our Histories

• *"How did our relationship*
• *come unstuck? What can*
I do to reconnect?"

The past is past. It happened. It is over and done with. And yet, there is a way in which the past still lives on. It lives on in us in terms of what we have become because of it. We bear the fruits of the past. Choices we made, actions we undertook, ideas we believed, and relationships we experienced all live on in us—for good and for ill.

There are things from the past we wish we could change. On one level, we cannot undo what has been done. But on another—the interior level—we can enter into a new relationship with the past.

For example, John's father was an abusive man. John could remember the atmosphere of fear in his childhood home. There was one incident in particular that summed up all of his feelings growing up. He came home late one night, thirty-five minutes past curfew. He was dependent on a friend for a ride and his friend wouldn't leave the party. John's father was waiting for him. John expected the lecture that he got—the cursing, the threats, the demeaning comments. What he didn't expect was the destruction. His father punished him by trashing his room—his safe haven—while John watched. His father ripped the posters off the wall, and broke the records he had so carefully collected. Even though John is grown now with a family of his own, he still feels torn up inside whenever he thinks of that night.

John needs to establish a new relationship with this incident, and his journal can help him to do so.
• First, the journal allows him to recall and write out in great detail the whole event. Often the act of making memories concrete robs them of some of their power over us. We bring them from the darkness into the light.
• Second, in his journal John can offer this incident to God in prayer and ask for healing. He can pray a prayer in which, in his imagination, he asks Jesus to stand with him on that fateful night, to be with him as he endures his father's shouts, and as his father vents his rage on his room. We cannot always predict where such prayers of imagination will take us, but it is not uncommon for great healing to emerge from them.
• Third, in his journal John can begin a dialogue with his father. This journal method (see p. 42) has great power to give us new insight into a relationship and to bring progress in stalled relationships.

It is not just relationships from the past that we must deal with. As you work with the various periods in your life, be on the lookout for any incidents, events, ideas, or behaviors that are still vivid. Where guilt, pain, or questions emerge, that is where our attention should be.

PART ONE/Learning to Journal

Session Overview

Growth involves dealing with the past so that you move beyond it into health and wholeness.

As you explore your past in your period work, you will come across issues that need resolution. In this session, you will learn a way to engage these issues directly by means of a journal dialogue. In so doing, you will often be given insight as to what is required in the present to defuse (or grow beyond) the past.

Telling Our Stories (15/20 minutes)

"People who need people . . ."

Life is relationship. We all have certain people who bring light and joy into our lives.

1. When you were a child, who was your best friend? Describe him or her.

2. Who is your best friend now (apart from your spouse)? Or describe what the ideal best friend would be like.

3. From the list below, what do you think are the two or three most impor-tant characteristics of a best friend?
   - ❏ a sense of humor
   - ❏ loyalty
   - ❏ an uncomplaining spirit
   - ❏ a deep faith
   - ❏ always available
   - ❏ common sense
   - ❏ a sympathetic ear
   - ❏ a fun spirit
   - ❏ an undemanding nature
   - ❏ common interests

The Journal Method (5 minutes)

Dialogue

If our aim is to understand our past relationships, we need a concrete way to get in touch with the inner shape of our lives. This is what the dialogue method of journaling provides for us.

The idea is simple: we frame an imaginary dialogue with a person. We "talk" to that person in our journal, writing out our conversation. In so doing, we come to a new understanding of our relationship with that person. This is not a very mysterious process. We know from experience that in conversation we work out our questions, we sort through our ideas until they are clear, and we realize things that we had not been aware of. Journal dialogues work in the same way.

Our imagination is a powerful tool for growth. Some people worry about the use of imagination—they believe that it is inferior to the intellect and that it is capable of being distorted. They forget that our imagination is as much a gift from God as our intellect is. And both intellect and imagination can be put to good use or to bad; both can be distorted. It depends on how we use them. God wants us to use both.

We can dialogue not only with people, but also with any aspect of our lives. Since this is an imaginary reconstruction anyway, it's possible to imagine a dialogue with our career ("Okay, you and I have got to talk because from my point of view, you are going nowhere . . ."). We can dialogue with incidents that have taken place in the world around us, with our bodies—we can dialogue with anything. The whole idea may sound strange until you try it. But you will be amazed at the insights that emerge.

These kinds of dialogues work, I am convinced, not because they mystically put us in touch with real entities, but because they allow us to access thoughts and feelings from our unconscious.

Dialogue categories include:
- Persons: past and present, living and dead, close or distant
- Projects to which you have given energy: creative works, a job or career, a business venture, a ministry
- Body (the physical side of life): injuries or illness, body parts, our size or shape, physical activities
- Events: things that happen to us, for good or ill, personal or societal
- Inner realities: dreams, emotions, values, our attitude toward God, spiritual experiences
- Ideas that grip us, move us, annoy us, challenge us

It is also useful to record our ordinary dialogue. You recall an important conversation during the day. Recording it (or snatches of it) in your journal allows you to reflect on the conversation. In your journal, you can try to extend the conversation or move it in a new direction through this dialogue technique—out of which new clarity may come.

The Journal Exercise (15/30 minutes)

Preparation:
- Get out your journal. Find a comfortable spot in which to journal. Date your journal. Entitle the entry: Dialogue with (fill-in-the-blank). File this in the Dialogue section of your journal.
- Go over the directions below that describe the journaling exercise.
- Do the focusing exercise, asking the Holy Spirit to lead you as you journal.
- Begin journaling, in silence, for the time allotted.

Process:
There are four parts to this exercise.

1. Select a person with whom to dialogue. Pick someone who matters to you, someone with whom you have an association, like a parent or an ex-friend who let you down. Pick a relationship in your past or present that needs a further step of development.

2. Describe the present state of your relationship in two to four paragraphs. What is positive about it? Negative? What is open? Hidden? What are our joys? Frustrations? Where do we stand now? In preparing these paragraphs, you may want to read over past journal entries connected to this person.

3. Enter into dialogue with the person. You do this by sitting in silence and imagining that you are with them. Begin a conversation in your mind. Listen to the response. Let the dialogue proceed. Write down the dialogue script as it unfolds. Record it without assessing what is said, while you remain in the imaginary dialogue. Your main focus needs to be on the dialogue, not on recording it.

4. Read over (aloud if possible) the dialogue script. As you do so, note your reactions and assessments in your journal.
   - What new things do you learn about this relationship?
   - What feelings are evoked?
   - What challenges to action are here?
   - What is the next step in your relationship?
   - How must you pray about this relationship?

Option: You can use this process to dialogue with events, projects, ideas, etc.

Journal Sharing (20/30 minutes)

When you finish journaling, discuss your findings with the group.

1. Explore the process of journaling:
   - What was the easiest part of the process for you? Why?
   - What was the most difficult part of the process for you? Why?
   - What new thing did you learn about how to journal?

2. Share your insights from the journal experience:
   - With whom did you dialogue (and why)?
   - What are some of the things you learned from the dialogue?
   - What new insights came from this process that you had not known or considered before?
   - How easy or difficult was the dialogue exercise for you? How else might you apply it?

3. Pray about this experience:
   - What single thing would you like the group to pray about?

Journaling Assignment (5 minutes)

During the next week:

- Read over all of the material in the chapter, including the excerpt from *Confessions* by Saint Augustine.

- Use the dialogue method to explore other aspects of the time period you have been investigating.

- Ask God to bring new insight into your life as a result of doing these dialogues. Pray that you will be able to apply what you learn.

- Discern what new insights you have into your unfolding story. What new things have you learned about the shape and character of your spiritual pilgrimage during the period you are exploring?

- Decide what you want to share with your group during the next session from your dialogue exercises.

Journal Readings

The *Confessions* by Saint Augustine is regarded as one of the greatest journals and a masterpiece of Western literature. The title has a double meaning: *confession* as praise to God (Augustine's words in this journal are addressed to God) and *confession* as admission of faults. Augustine is disarmingly candid about his life. In retrospect, he is amazed when he considers the ways that God has been active in his life. What follows is a famous excerpt: the account of his conversion.

(28) From a hidden depth a profound self-examination had dredged up a heap of all my misery and set it "in the sight of my heart" (Ps. 18:15). That precipitated a vast storm bearing a massive downpour of tears. To pour it all out with the accompanying groans, I got up from beside Alypius (solitude seemed to me more appropriate for the business of weeping), and I moved further away to ensure that even his presence put no inhibition upon me. He sensed that this was my condition at that moment. I think I may have said something which made it clear that the sound of my voice was already choking with tears. So I stood up while in profound astonishment he remained where we were sitting. I threw myself down somehow under a certain figtree, and let my tears flow freely. Rivers streamed from my eyes, a sacrifice acceptable to you (Ps. 50:19), and (though not in these words, yet in this sense) I repeatedly said to you: "How long, O Lord? How long, Lord, will you be angry to the uttermost? Do not be mindful of our old iniquities." (Ps. 6:4). For I felt my past to have a grip on me. It uttered wretched cries: "How long, how long is it to be?" "Tomorrow, tomorrow." "Why not now? Why not an end to my impure life in this very hour?"

(29) As I was saying this and weeping in the bitter agony of my heart, suddenly I heard a voice from the nearby house chanting as if it might be a boy or a girl (I do not know which), saying and repeating over and over again "Pick up and read, pick up and read." At once my countenance changed, and I began to think intently whether there might be some sort of children's game in which such a chant is used. But I could not remember having heard of one. I checked the flood of tears and stood up. I interpreted it solely as a divine command to me to open the book and read the first chapter I might find. For I had heard how Antony happened to be present at the gospel reading, and took it as an admonition addressed to himself when the words were read: "Go, sell all you have, give to the poor, and you shall have treasure in heaven; and come, follow me" (Matt. 19:21). By such an inspired utterance he was immediately "converted to you" (Ps. 50:15). So I hurried back to the place where Alypius was sitting. There I had put down the book of the apostle when I got up. I seized it, opened it and in silence read the first passage on which my eyes lit: "Not in riots and drunken parties, not in eroticism and indecencies, not in strife and rivalry, but put on the Lord Jesus Christ and make no provision for the flesh in its lusts" (Rom. 13:13–14).

I neither wished nor needed to read further. At once, with the last words of this sentence, it was as if a light of relief from all anxiety flooded into my heart. All the shadows of doubt were dispelled. [1]

PART TWO/Bible Study

Session Overview

Peter is a man with whom we can identify. We identify with his energy, his brashness, his strong feelings, his deep commitments, his spontaneity. We can relax a bit with Peter and remember our own misguided enthusiasm. We can admit our moments of brashness. We can feel okay about our strong feelings. Barnabas, Paul, and Ruth are role models for us (which we desperately need). Peter is a reminder that Jesus loves imperfect people like us. Of course, Peter is a role model too. He can inspire us to step out and be bold, to respond strongly, and to grow from our mistakes.

Look at incidents in Peter's life and consider what his journal might have contained.

Telling Our Stories (15/20 minutes)

Energy

Peter lived life with gusto. He never went into anything half-heartedly. It was his style to jump in enthusiastically with both feet and with strong feelings.

1. Who is the most energetic person you have known or know about (i.e., a teacher, a relative, a sibling, a friend, a co-worker, a sports figure, a TV character, or someone you have read about)? Describe him or her.

2. Have you ever been involved in a project or mission where you were very energetic and enthusiastic? Describe it.

3. What is the biggest "goof" you ever made? What did you learn? How did you "recover"?

Exploring the Text (20/35 minutes)

Selections from the life of Peter

Read through each of the following passages, and discuss them using the questions below. (Remember the option on p. 24.)

1. Peter walks on water: Matthew 14:22–33
   - Describe the variety of emotions felt by the Twelve. What did they feel in the midst of the enthusiastic crowd? When the storm came? When they spotted Jesus walking on the water? When Jesus revealed himself to them? When they saw Peter step out of the boat? Walk on water? Sink? When Peter and Jesus got into the boat and the wind died?
   - How do you suppose Peter described the experience of walking on water in his journal?

2. Peter at Caesarea Philippi: Mark 8:27–9:1
   - What is the best guess on the part of the crowds as to who Jesus was? In contrast, what have the Twelve concluded?
   - What kind of Messiah is Jesus?
   - In his journal, how might Peter have described both the excitement and the confusion of that day at Caesarea Philippi?

3. Peter betrays Jesus: Matthew 26:31–35,69–75
   - What does Jesus predict? What is Peter's vow?
   - How does Peter betray Jesus?
   - What might Peter have written regarding the contrast between his vow that he alone would never disown Jesus, and his subsequent and vigorous denial of Jesus?

4. Peter heals the crippled beggar: Acts 3:1–26
   - Describe Peter's encounter with the beggar and the various responses to it.
   - What is the central point of Peter's impromptu "sermon" in vv. 12–26?
   - How might Peter have described this incident and the subsequent events in his journal (see also Acts 4)?

5. Peter's vision: Acts 10:1–29,44–48
   - Describe the visions of Cornelius and Peter, and the meaning of each.
   - What great new event in the development of the early church was Peter at the center of here?
   - In his journal, how might Peter have explained the new breakthrough in his understanding that took place in this incident?

6. Peter escapes from prison: Acts 12:1–18
   - What does this passage tell you about the character of the early church in Jerusalem and the climate in which it existed?
   - What happens to Peter?
   - What did Peter make of this incident in his journal?

Responding to the Text (20/30 minutes)

In your story:

1. Describe an incident in your life when you took a risk or stepped out in faith into a new but uncertain venture. What happened? What are you called upon to risk now?

2. How did you discover who Jesus really was (as opposed to cultural ideas about him)? How did you respond to what you discovered?

3. As you look back over your life, can you recall a time when you betrayed a friend, a principle, a promise, a conviction, or a dream? Discuss that experience. Or talk about a time when you were betrayed and what that experience did to you.

4. Describe an incident in which you saw the power of God work through you. This does not have to be an experience like the one the beggar had with Peter. It could be a kind word that restored a child's confidence, a prayer that was answered, a decision not to give in to temptation. All qualify as events in which God worked in and through us.

5. What prejudices have you faced in your life, and how have you overcome them?

6. Can you recall a situation when you had to be bold or brave, or when you faced opposition because of what you believed? How did you feel? What happened?

Journal Assignment (5 minutes)

In your journal, continue to explore the story of Peter. Be attentive to the parallels between his story and your story. In your journal, explore further the incidents in your life that you recalled during the small group discussion. Be alert to new insights about your past that emerge by examining your experiences in light of Scripture. Use the story of Peter as a way to recall other incidents in your past. If you find it useful, write "the journal of Peter" as a way of understanding his story in Scripture.

Background Notes

- **feeding of the 5,000:** The incident in which Peter walks on water is preceded by the feeding of the 5,000. The crowds were so amazed and overwhelmed by what Jesus did that they sought to make him king immediately (see John 6:14–15). Jesus deals with the crowds—he tries to defuse a situation that could cripple his ministry (by giving people a misleading impression of what kind of Messiah he was). Meanwhile, he sends the disciples off, so that they won't be infected with this messianic fever. The disciples never imagine that Jesus will join them by walking across the water.
- **fourth watch:** 3:00–6:00 a.m.
- **the Christ:** The Greek term for "Messiah." The popular view of the Messiah was that he would be an invincible military figure who would defeat the Romans and establish Jerusalem as the capital of the world. Jesus, however, came as the suffering servant who would die for the sins of the world. Once the Twelve recognized that he was the long-expected Messiah, he could begin teaching them about the kind of Messiah he was.
- **he rebuked Peter:** Peter had understood who Jesus was, but not what kind of Messiah he would be. Peter is shocked by what Jesus says. In his mind, Messiahs do not suffer and die. So Peter rebukes Jesus privately for his "erroneous" teachings, and earns a rebuke from Jesus in return.
- **the Lord's Supper:** This was the Passover meal eaten by Jewish families in remembrance of Israel's deliverance from Egypt. Jesus takes two of the elements from this meal (bread and wine) and uses them to institute this new celebration in which Christians recall Jesus' atoning death for them. It is in this context that both Judas' and Peter's betrayal is set.
- **you will all fall away:** It was not just Peter who denied Jesus. Judas betrayed him to the Jewish officials, and the other ten fled into the night.
- **Peter's recovery:** Between Peter's denial of Jesus and his bold declaration in Jerusalem, Peter encounters the resurrected Jesus. It is there that Peter experienced the love and forgiveness of his Lord (see Mark 16:7; Luke 24:34; 1 Corinthians 15:5).
- **the Temple courtyards:** Peter's encounter with the crippled beggar and the subsequent events all took place in the spacious courtyards of the Temple in Jerusalem.
- **impure, unclean:** Jewish dietary laws were very strict. In his vision, Peter was asked to eat what was forbidden. He cannot bring himself to do so. The vision prepares Peter to accept the Gentiles who come to his house, also something a devout Jew wouldn't have done in the first century.

---

[1] *Confessions* by Saint Augustine, trans. by Henry Chadwick (New York: Oxford University Press, 1992).

Chapter Five

Using Journals to Realize Our Future

"The future has great power over us. When it is filled with dread, we retreat into the past; but when it is filled with hope, we stride forward."

I once had a colleague who taught a course on "The History of the Future." Now of course, you can't discuss the "history" of something that has not yet happened. So the way he taught the course was to look at current trends and speculate where they were leading. This is how we can approach our future: by getting in touch with our past and noticing the trajectories we find that point into the future.

For example, when reflecting on your past, you remember that as a kid you were always building things: birdhouses, railroad villages, forts. In high school you got A's in shop class. You went on to get a degree in civil engineering. Sometimes the trajectory in your life is clear.

But at other times the trajectories are not so obvious. For example, as you scan the past periods of your life, you find that people are important in each period. In fact, different people define different periods for you. Furthermore, in each instance you are in a relationship where you help key people. In light of this, as you consider the ministry or career to which God is calling you, it makes sense to go into a helping profession of some kind. But you may miss this fact, since "helping others" is just something you do. You hardly notice. You assume everybody is like this.

When we are clear about the direction in which God has been nudging us, we can make sensible decisions: about training, about lay ministry, about how to structure our lives, about how to use our time, about where and how to live. For the Christian, it is important to become what God wants us to become. We have a strong and curious sense that our lives are supposed to matter, that we have a part to play in the unfolding drama of God's kingdom, and that who we become is important. The challenge is to find the future God has for us. This is where journals can be a help.

When we have an idea of what God has done in the past, we are better able to make choices for the future. When we're given the option of going in various directions, a clear sense of how we've been shaped and gifted by God makes it easier to choose. What we want to choose is God's future.

PART ONE/Learning to Journal

Session Overview

One way to discern God's future for you is to pay attention to the past. Your future is often hidden in your past.

In this session, you will learn two ways of journaling. In the first, the Crossroads exercise, you discern new possibilities in your future by finding past roads you did not (or could not) follow at the time. These may be new roads that you can now walk along. In the second, the Patterns exercise, you reflect on the past to discern who you have become and, therefore, to know where you should go.

Telling Our Stories (15/20 minutes)

"Some day . . ."

Most of us dream about the future: what we will become, where we will go, what we will do. These dreams about the future are almost always bright and wonderful.

1. When you were a child, what did you dream of becoming?
   - ❏ a professional (doctor, lawyer, dentist, minister, accountant)
   - ❏ a service worker (firefighter, police officer, ambulance driver)
   - ❏ a business person (CEO, accountant, boss, salesperson)
   - ❏ a wanderer (scuba instructor, beach bum, explorer)
   - ❏ a parent   ❏ an athlete
   - ❏ an entertainer   ❏ a recluse
   - ❏ a teacher   ❏ other: _____

2. By your senior year in high school, how had your plans changed? Why?

3. Which of your career dreams, if any, have you realized? Which do you hope to realize in the future? What new dreams do you have?

The Journal Method (5 minutes)

Crossroads

We are forced to make choices. Contrary to the ad, it's not possible "to have it all." Some choices are small and of little consequence: to order fish or chicken at the restaurant; to pick an action video or a comedy. Other choices have major consequences: to go to college or to start work; to take drugs or to stay clean. The big choices—the crossroads choices—move us in new and decisive directions.

For example, Janet was just finishing junior college and wanted to go to art school. In her two years of college, it had become clear to her what she loved to do. It had also become clear that she wanted to spend the rest of her life with Pete, and he wanted to marry her. Janet was at a crossroads. She could get married or she could go to art school. She could not do both. There was not enough money. So Janet chose to get married. She would delay art school eighteen months until Pete finished his degree. But Janet got pregnant in their first year of marriage, so art school was put on hold.

We make a number of choices like the one Janet made. Often we realize the magnitude or the implications of what we've chosen. Most of the time, we forget about the option that we didn't choose.

But there may come a time when we can go back to a crossroads and start down the road that we didn't take. At the time, that road was closed to us. But now the time has come to go in that direction.

This is one way to assess where to go in the future: by remembering crossroads from the past and discerning whether it is now time to explore the road not chosen.[1]

Janet is now forty-two years old and the mother of three. The children are older and independent. Pete is a high school principal. Janet feels that the time has finally come to take the other road. She will get her art degree.

Patterns

There is a second way of working with the past in order to get a sense of the future. In this exercise, scan the work you have done in the various periods in your life, and look for the following:

- Skills: What are you good at? What have you been trained in?
- Ministry: What forms of ministry have you tried? Enjoyed? Desire to participate in?
- Success: Where have you found success in your life?
- Failure: Where have you been less than successful? (It is good to know what not to pursue.)
- Joy: What brings you joy in life?
- Longings: What have you always wanted to do?

As you explore each of these areas, you will develop a deeper appreciation of the patterns in your life. Thus you will have a better sense of where you can go in the future.

The Journal Exercise (15/30 minutes)

Preparation:

- Get out your journal. Find a comfortable spot in which to journal. Date your journal. Entitle the entry: Crossroads. File this in the History section of your journal.
- Go over the directions below that describe the journaling exercise.
- Do the focusing exercise, asking the Holy Spirit to lead you as you journal.
- Begin journaling, in silence, for the time allotted.

Process:

There are three parts to the Crossroads exercise:

1. **Identify a Crossroads event:** Go back to a particular period in your life and look for crossroads. Scan your reflections on different periods until you find such an event. Once you have identified the event you wish to explore, write up to three paragraphs describing the Crossroads as clearly as you can.

2. **Explore the road not taken by using your imagination:** Picture yourself back at the place where you made the choice, but this time choose to go in the other direction. Imagine what would have happened. Watch your life unfold as you walk this new road. Write down your imaginative journey in your journal.

3. **Consider your life direction:** To recall past crossroads is not the same as choosing to walk an untraveled road. In fact, most of the time the other road is still closed to us. We've lost interest. We have become different people. We no longer have the desire. Or the option is no longer available to us. But sometimes we come upon a road we still need to walk. What we need to know is whether this is the time to do it, and that this is God's will. Reflect on the following questions:
   - Why does this road still hold interest for you?
   - What price would you have to pay to walk it?
   - What good would come from walking it?
   - How would this affect your life, especially your relationships?
   - What is your sense when you pray about this?

Option: You may be at a Crossroads now. You can use this exercise to explore these options. Instead of doing the above exercise:

- Describe your options as clearly as possible.
- In your mind, imagine yourself as you walk down one of the roads. What might this future look like? Now go back in your imagination to the other option, and consider what life would be like if you chose it.
- Review your journal accounts of walking down each road. What new insights do you gain?

Journal Sharing (20/30 minutes)

When you finish journaling, discuss your findings with the group.

1. Explore the process of journaling:
   - What was the easiest part of the process for you? Why?
   - What was the most difficult part of the process for you? Why?
   - What new thing did you learn about how to journal?

2. Share your insights from the journal experience:
   - What Crossroads event did you investigate? Was it easy or hard to find this event? Why were you drawn to it?
   - What happened when you explored the road you didn't take?
   - Is this untraveled road still interesting to you? If so, is now the time to travel it? If not now, when?
   - How did you answer the questions in the "Consider your life direction" portion of the exercise?

3. Pray about this experience:
   - What single thing would you like the group to pray about?

Journaling Assignment (5 minutes)

During the next week:

- Read over all of the material in the chapter, including the excerpt from *Markings* by Dag Hammarskjöld.

- Work on the issue of untraveled roads. Explore other time periods with this question in mind. Investigate different roads that appear to have some potential for you right now. Do the Patterns exercise (see p. 53).

- Ask God to guide you as you reflect on the future. Ask God to protect you from running off in the wrong direction, and to reveal the right one to you. Pray that you will be able to apply what you learn.

- Discern what new insights you have into your unfolding story. What new things have you learned about the shape and character of your spiritual pilgrimage by examining these untraveled roads?

- Decide what you want to share with the group during the next session from your Crossroads exercise.

Journal Readings

Dag Hammarskjöld, who was Secretary General of the U.N. at the time of his death, considered his diary "as a sort of 'White Book' concerning my negotiations with myself—and with God." The diary is curious in that it contains no references to his work as a diplomat, no comment on the famous people he met nor on the historical events he participated in. Rather, it is the story of his slow movement from despair to faith in God. W. H. Auden, who worked on the translation of *Markings*, commented that in reading it "one has the privilege of being in contact with a great, good, and lovable man."

4.8.59 To have humility is to experience reality, not in relation to ourselves, but in its sacred independence. It is to see, judge, and act from the point of rest in ourselves. Then, how much disappears, and all that remains falls into place.

In the point of rest at the centre of our being, we encounter a world where all things are at rest in the same way. Then a tree becomes a mystery, a cloud, a revelation, each man a cosmos of whose riches we can only catch glimpses. The life of simplicity is simple, but it opens to us a book in which we never get beyond the first syllable.

Easter, 1960 Forgiveness breaks the chain of causality because he who "forgives" you—out of love—takes upon himself the consequences of what you have done. Forgiveness, therefore, always entails a sacrifice.

The price you must pay for your own liberation through another's sacrifice, is that you in turn must be willing to liberate in the same way, irrespective of the consequences to yourself.

Whitsunday, 1961 I don't know Who—or what—put the question, I don't know when it was put. I don't even remember answering. But at some moment I did answer Yes to Someone—or Something—and from that hour I was certain that existence is meaningful and that, therefore, my life, in self-surrender, had a goal.

From that moment I have known what it means "not to look back" and "to take no thought for the morrow."

Led by the Ariadne's thread of my answer through the labyrinth of Life, I came to a time and place where I realised that the Way leads to a triumph which is a catastrophe, and to a catastrophe which is a triumph, that the price for committing one's life would be reproach, and that the only elevation possible to man lies in the depths of humiliation. After that, the word "courage" lost its meaning, since nothing could be taken from me.

As I continued along the Way, I learned, step by step, word by word, that behind every saying in the Gospels, stands one man and one man's experience. Also behind the prayer that the cup might pass from him and his promise to drink it. Also behind each of the words from the Cross. [2]

PART TWO/Bible Study

Session Overview

Mary and Martha are well-known as two sisters with different personalities. Martha was ordered and organized: a "J" in Myers–Briggs parlance, while Mary was more spontaneous and more relational: a clear "P." But there is more to these two women than their different approaches to life. They (along with their brother Lazarus) were friends of Jesus, and they were caught up in unimaginable events when Jesus raised their brother from the dead.

Look at incidents in the lives of Mary and Martha and consider what their journals might have contained.

Telling Our Stories (15/20 minutes)

Opposites

We are not all alike—thank God! Often it is our differences that energize a relationship—not our similarities.

1. What "type" of person are you? Look over the following contrasts and check your preference of the two options:
   * When shopping do you:
     ❐ choose carefully?   ❐ choose impulsively?
   * Do you prefer:
     ❐ finishing a task?   ❐ doing different tasks?
   * At a party, are you busy:
     ❐ organizing the food?   ❐ talking to everyone?
   * A friend says, "Let's go to the beach." Do you:
     ❐ check your calendar?   ❐ say, "Let's go!"?
   * Do you consider yourself:
     ❐ organized?   ❐ spontaneous?

   If you checked more items in the first column than the second, you are most likely a "J"; that is, a person who is organized, orderly, takes control, and is uncomfortable with too much spontaneity. If you checked more items in the second column, you are most likely a "P"; that is, a person who responds to a situation rather than organizes it, is comfortable with whatever happens, and has a "wait and see" attitude.

2. What are the benefits you see of being the "type" of person you are? What are the drawbacks?

3. Think about your close relationships. Do you tend to have friends of the same or different "type"?

Exploring the Text (20/35 minutes)

Selections from the lives of Mary and Martha

Read through each of the following passages, and discuss them using the questions below.

1. Jesus visits Martha and Mary: Luke 10:38–42
   • Describe the different personalities of Mary and Martha.
   • How would the accounts of this particular day differ in the journals of each of these women?

2. The death of Lazarus: John 11:1–16
   • Lazarus is ill. What are the hopes and expectations of the sisters in this situation? What is Jesus' agenda? What are the fears and needs of the disciples?
   • What do you suppose Mary and Martha wrote in their journals as they mourned their brother's death and waited for Jesus?

3. Jesus comforts Mary and Martha: John 11:17–37
   • How does Martha respond to Jesus? How does Mary respond? The Jews who were comforting the sisters?
   • What do Jesus' pronouncements and his actions tell you about him?
   • What might Mary and Martha have written about Jesus in their journals after he arrived at their home?

4. Jesus raises Lazarus from the dead: John 11:38–44
   • How would an onlooker have described the raising of Lazarus?
   • What do you think it was like for Lazarus to die and then four days later to come back to life? Would he have been pleased or pained?
   • Describe what Mary and Martha might have written in their journals about the raising of their brother from the dead.

5. The aftermath: John 11:45–57
   • How do the officials and religious leaders respond to the raising of Lazarus? Why?
   • What happens to Jesus because of this?
   • What might the sisters have written about the aftermath of their brother's return for them and for Jesus?

6. Mary anoints Jesus' feet: John 12:1–11
   • How did the various people respond to this situation: Mary? Judas? Jesus? The crowd?
   • What was the meaning of Mary's act?
   • What might Mary have written in her journal about anointing Jesus' feet?

Responding to the Text (20/30 minutes)

In your story:

1. Identify various incidents in which your tendency to organize—or to act spontaneously—produced good or bad results. Talk about one of these incidents.

2. Have you ever endured a serious illness of a friend or family member? What was the daily waiting like? What did you learn from that situation?

3. Whose deaths have you experienced? Which was the hardest for you? How did you express your grief?

4. What experiences, if any, have you had of "resurrection": of a person miraculously escaping a fatal accident or disease; of a hopeless situation turning out all right; of unexpected good news?

5. Have you been involved in any modern movement—the civil rights movement, the counterculture, the peace movement? How were you personally affected by these events?

6. Have you ever done something really extravagant for someone else, or for some higher purpose or goal? Describe it.

Journal Assignment (5 minutes)

In your journal, continue to explore the story of Mary and Martha. Be attentive to the parallels between their story and your story. In your journal, explore further the incidents in your life that you recalled during the small group discussion. Be alert to new insights about your past that emerge by examining your experiences in light of Scripture. Use the story of these two sisters as a way of recalling other incidents in your past. If you find it useful, write "the journal of Mary and Martha" as a way of understanding their story in Scripture.

Background Notes

- **a village:** Mary and Martha lived in the village of Bethany, located about two miles from Jerusalem.
- **"Lord, the one you love is sick":** By now, it was well established that Jesus was a powerful and effective healer. The sisters expected that Jesus would heal his good friend Lazarus. In fact, Jesus will heal him— but not in the way the sisters expect. First Lazarus must die.

- **stoning:** At this point in his ministry, Jesus had many enemies. His disciples recognized that he would put himself in danger if he went to Jerusalem. It was the religious establishment's center and the place where Jesus' enemies had the most power.
- **four days:** It was a common belief in those days that the soul lingered near the body for three days and then departed. Since Lazarus had been dead for four days, it meant that he was now irrevocably dead. There was no hope of resuscitation.
- **mourning:** When a friend or family member died, he or she was buried on the same day. A week of intense mourning followed. The bereaved sat on the floor of their home, and friends came to comfort them.
- **"I am the resurrection and the life":** It is not just that Jesus has the power to raise people from the dead and to give them new life. In his essence, Jesus himself is resurrection and life.
- **wrapped with strips of linen:** Bodies were buried in caves with stones at the entrance to keep animals and thieves out. The body was wrapped and left for a year, after this the bones were collected and put in a box. After four days, decomposition would be underway. For Lazarus, it would have been a struggle to emerge from the tomb (wrapped up as he was).
- **Sanhedrin:** The Jewish high court, which consisted of the elders, chief priests, and teachers of the law. It had seventy-one members. The high priest presided over its meetings. The Roman rulers gave this group great authority over the affairs of the Jews.
- **Caiaphas:** He was the high priest from approximately A.D. 18–36. His main concern in this was political, not whether Jesus was from God or not. He feared that a mass movement sparked by Jesus would lead to a Roman response that would put the whole nation in jeopardy.
- **Jesus would die for the nation:** In fact, Caiaphas was correct in his prediction—though not in the way he imagined. Jesus died that year for the sins of the nation (and indeed, for the sins of the whole world). Jesus' death did not, however, solve the political problems that the Jews faced. In fact, the nation perished in A.D. 70 at the hands of the Romans.
- **nard:** a plant from which fragrant oil was extracted.
- **poured it on Jesus' feet:** This was an extraordinary act in many ways. For one thing, such perfume was very expensive and normally only a small amount was used. Mary poured a whole pint on Jesus' feet. For another thing, Mary poured the oil on his feet, not on his head (as was the custom). Then she wiped it off with her own hair and washed his feet, assuming the role of a servant. A respectable woman kept her hair bound; she would not have let it down in public like this. All of this was quite fitting, however, since Jesus would not receive a proper burial when he was killed a few days later.

---

[1] This is Progoff's phrase for this exercise.

[2] *Markings* by Dag Hammarskjöld, trans. by Leif Sjöberg and W. H. Auden (London: Faber and Faber, 1964).

Chapter Six

Exploring Our Inner World

*"So murky; so hidden, yet so potent.
To know myself from within ... so
powerful, so difficult, so vital."*

To speak of an inner world is to recognize that who we are is not just what we do. We are what we feel, what we dream, what we imagine, what we long for, what we hear God saying to us—all of this is a vital part of who we are. Journals are a powerful tool for exploring this inner world.

Take feelings—we all feel. We differ, however, in our ability to identify and express our feelings. Men, in particular, often have a difficult time with the emotional side of life. Most of them weren't allowed to express their feelings when they were younger. When it comes to the emotional side of life, journals allow us to do two things: to identify our feelings and then to express them in appropriate ways. The first step in our journals is to identify what we're feeling, rather than let vague emotions swirl around inside us. Ignoring, denying, or suppressing our feelings is not a healthy practice. The second step is to learn how to express our emotions, especially the negative ones. Sometimes it is simply enough to write down what we're feeling, or to write a letter that we will never send. At other times, however, we'll need to express our feelings directly to the people concerned. Journals allow us to think through how to deal with our emotions.

And what about our dreams? Everybody dreams, though we differ in our ability to remember them. Dreams are often a clue to what is going on in our inner lives. They "express the outward circumstances of a person's life, his current problems and fears, and also the hopes and goals toward which he is consciously planning. In addition, however, dreams reflect the deeper-than-conscious goals that are trying to unfold in a person's life . . . ." Ira Progoff has pointed out that dreams also bring to the fore destructive patterns and purposes in a person's life, of which he or she is unaware.[1]

God can also speak to us through dreams. This is certainly the case in the Bible. For example, our Lord's own life was saved by Joseph's willingness to pay attention to his dreams (Matthew 2:19–23).

Along with our dreams, there are all of those images, reflections, thoughts, and intuitions that make up the substance of our inner world. We can learn a lot about ourselves by bringing these things to the surface, identifying them, and writing them down. Then we can own our inner world, deal with it, accept or reject it, process it, and pray about it.

PART ONE/Learning to Journal

Session Overview

A journal is a useful tool for getting in touch with the many dimensions of the inner life: feelings, dreams, reflections, intuitions, creativity, and the sense of God's presence.

Two ways of journaling are suggested in this session. In the first, the Creativity exercise, we try a simple exercise to evoke a creative response. In the second, the Dreams exercise, we work with our dream record to find insights that will be useful in our growth.

Telling Our Stories (15/20 minutes)

Creating

Everyone is creative. We can't help it. We are made in the image of God, and God is creative. So our creativity is a faint echo of his.

1. When you were a child, in what way(s) did you express your creativity?
   - ❏ with my hands
   - ❏ through what I said
   - ❏ through my singing
   - ❏ through my mind
   - ❏ in my play
   - ❏ in my relationships

2. Which creative outlet(s) do you like most? Which do you long to do? Which area is unexplored?

❏ painting	❏ poetry	❏ dance
❏ drawing	❏ sculpture	❏ relationships
❏ storytelling	❏ writing	❏ decorating
❏ music	❏ media	❏ designing
❏ cooking	❏ composing	❏ sewing
❏ child rearing	❏ video	❏ wood/metalworking
❏ crafts	❏ journaling	❏ other: _____

3. What have you created that has given you the most satisfaction?

The Journal Method (5 minutes)

Two journal methods are described in this session. Choose one of them for your time of journaling.

The Creative Spirit

You are a creative person. You can't help it—you are made in the image of God, and he is, in his nature, a creative being. The problem is that we don't always recognize our creativity. Your journal is a good vehicle through which to discover and explore your creativity.

Creativity can be revealed in a variety of ways. Part of the challenge is to discover the vehicle that best expresses your creative spirit—pottery, poetry, or painting, for example. Do not be deterred by the thought that you need to master a technique. Just begin. No one else will see your journal. Pick the creative outlet that appeals to you most. Be playful, and don't put any pressure on yourself to "be creative."

If *words* appeal to you, play with them. Write a poem, reconstruct a conversation, articulate an important thought, or write a letter. Put words to paper. See where this leads. Don't critique what you produce. Editing and reworking will come later.

If *images and shapes* appeal to you, start sketching. Draw a face, copy a design, doodle, sketch a cartoon. Or simply let lines flow from your pen. See what happens.

Another aspect of creativity is *content*. It's not merely *how* you express yourself, but *what* you express. What really matters to you? What do you have to say? Why? To whom? Wrestle with what matters to you. The combination of form and content is what creativity is all about.

Dealing with Dreams

The first step in dealing with dreams is to remember them. If recalling dreams is difficult for you, then you need to make plans before you go to sleep. This will involve several steps: First, tell yourself over and over again as you go to sleep, "I want to remember my dreams." Second, put a pen and some paper beside your bed so that when you wake up, you can immediately jot down whatever dream you recall. Third, set your alarm clock twenty minutes earlier than normal. This usually ensures that you will wake up in the middle of a dream.

The next step is exploring your dreams. It's best if you work with a series of dreams which have been recorded over time in your journal. Don't worry about interpreting them; simply make note of what you remember. As you read over the record of your dreams, be alert to impressions and insights. Are there recurring images? Do meanings jump out at you? What do the dreams make you feel? What connections do you sense between the dreams and your waking life? In other words, use dreams as clues to help you understand your inner life.[2]

The Journal Exercise (15/30 minutes)

Preparation:
- Get out your journal. Find a comfortable spot in which to journal. Date your journal. Entitle the entry: Creativity or Dreams (depending upon which exercise you want to explore). File this in either the Musings or Dreams section of your journal.
- Follow the directions below for your journaling exercise.
- Do the focusing exercise, asking the Holy Spirit to lead you as you journal.
- Begin journaling, in silence, for the time allotted.

Process:
Option 1: Creativity exercise
1. Read Psalm 23. Do this slowly, two or three times, until you begin to get a feel for what is being said.
2. When you feel ready, express Psalm 23 in a different format:
   - Paraphrase it from your present situation, or from the viewpoint of a person who is dying; or
   - Do a sketch (abstract or realistic) that captures the sense of the psalm; or
   - Write a poem about it; have a conversation with the Lord; outline a short story based on this psalm; or
   - Express it in music: write lyrics or the music; explain how you would express it if you were writing a symphony; or
   - Create a collage: paste together clippings from magazines which capture the sense of the psalm; or
   - Respond in your own creative way to the psalm.

After you complete the exercise, describe in your journal what the creative process was like for you.

Option 2: Dreams exercise
In order to do this exercise, you need to have at least one dream in your dream log that you can work with. It is better if you have a series of dreams.
1. Review the dreams—slowly, thoughtfully, prayerfully. Record your impressions, thoughts, and questions as you do so.
2. Give the dream or dream sequence a title (what the dream is all about). Describe the central themes. Next, describe the emotional tone of the dreams. Finally, identify any questions that have been raised for you.[3]
3. Holding the dream log and your work in the Daily and History sections side by side, identify any links you see. How does your inner life relate to your external life?

Journal Sharing (20/30 minutes)

When you finish journaling, discuss your findings with the group.

1. Explore the process of journaling:
   • What was the easiest part of the process for you? Why?
   • What was the most difficult part of the process for you? Why?
   • What new thing did you learn about how to journal?

2. Share your insights from the journal experience:
   • Which exercise did you do: the Creativity or the Dreams exercise? Why did you select it?

   • For those who did the Creativity exercise:
      Which creative outlet did you choose to explore? Why?
      Talk about the results.
      What did you learn about creativity? About your potential as a creative person?

   • For those who did the Dreams exercise:
      How many dreams did you consider?
      Talk about your dreams and the insights you gathered from them.
      What did you learn about the use of dreams in exploring your inner life?

   • What new aspects of your story have you uncovered?

3. Pray about this experience:
   • What single thing would you like the group to pray about?

Journaling Assignment (5 minutes)

During the next week:

• Read over all of the material in the chapter, including the excerpt from Jim Elliot's journal.
• Explore your creativity. Identify past experiences of creativity. Try new and inventive responses to Scripture (or to incidents in your life which you want to express).
• Explore your dream life. If you have not recorded any (or many) dreams, try to do so in the week ahead. Use the dreams you remember with the Dream exercise described above.
• Ask God to help you develop your creativity.
• Discern what new insights you have into your unfolding story. What new things have you learned about who you are?
• Decide what you want to share with your group during the next session from these exercises. You might want to share a creative piece with the group, but remember that you will have only two minutes.

Journal Readings

Jim Elliot not only used his journal to reflect on his life, but he also used it
as a tool for creative reflection on the Bible.

> *October 6/2 Corinthians 1*
> *Second Corinthians 1 was my morning meditation. Stirred to sober wonder at*
> *what, or rather who, shall be my glorying in the day of Jesus Christ? O Lord,*
> *how little deliverance I have wrought in the earth when compared with all*
> *Thy lavish promises of fruit. God grant me effectiveness in life and balance.*
> *Read some Nietzsche this afternoon. He uses constantly the idea of "some-*
> *thing over there"—the man beyond—the "ubermensch." Dreadful contrast*
> *he makes with my heavenly prophet, but he points up, not in the same direc-*
> *tion. This while reading:*
>
> *Body is not bad.*
> *Only to him who think it everything,*
> *To him it is very bad.*
> *Immanuel, what burden Thine*
> *To bear a body among men*
> *Who thought their body all?*
> > *How long e'er Spirit conquer Body?*
> > *E'er Body finds its frenzied joy*
> > *In slavery to Spirit?*
> *What is this?*
> *The greatest of Thy giving*
> *Was not Thy giving*
> *But Thy taking from us,*
> *With us, Body,*
> *Son of Man.*
> *Without this taking*
> *There would be no giving.*
> > *Lo, all our generations say,*
> > *"Our bodies suffice us not.*
> > *We lack not strong bodies,*
> > *We look not for beautiful, delicate bodies,*
> > *We want control of both."*
> *In Thee, Immanuel,*
> *We spat on Spirit*
> *And petted Body.*
> *And still we drink deep of Body*
> *And love him well; for,*
> *Though he masters us,*
> *As in wine, so in Body*
> *Do we tingle.*
> > *How long e'er Spirit conquer Body,*
> > *E'er Body finds its frenzied joy*
> > *In slavery to Spirit?* [4]

PART TWO/Bible Study

Session Overview

Joseph, the husband of Mary and the stepfather of Jesus, is an important figure in the Bible who remains largely in the background. If it had not been for his faithful obedience to the revelation of God, Jesus' early life would have been in jeopardy. When Jesus was growing up, Joseph was obviously an important figure. However, except for one brief appearance when Jesus is at the Temple, Joseph is never mentioned. By the time Jesus is an adult, Joseph has disappeared altogether. When reference is made to Jesus' family, it is to his mother Mary and to his brothers and sisters. Joseph was probably dead by that time. Joseph was an ordinary and decent man, caught up in great and cosmic events. He played his part in the background, quietly and faithfully. It is an ordinary life lived in extraordinary circumstances. We who also lead ordinary lives can learn much about faithful obedience from Joseph.

Look at incidents in Joseph's life and consider what his journal might have contained.

Telling Our Stories (15/20 minutes)

Fixing Things

Paul was an intellectual, Peter was an activist, Barnabas was an encourager, and Joseph was a craftsman. Paul thought, Peter acted, Barnabas connected emotionally, and Joseph fixed things. Interestingly, there are probably more of us like Joseph than like any of the other three.

1. When it comes to fixing a leaky faucet or a broken chair, how do you rate? Give an example of your home repair skills.
   - ❑ all thumbs
   - ❑ watch out—disaster ahead!
   - ❑ where's the phone book?
   - ❑ I'll try, but who knows?
   - ❑ competent but nervous
   - ❑ confident
   - ❑ step aside—let me at it!
   - ❑ I'll need some new tools

2. Who's the most interesting (or competent) craftsperson you've known? What could he or she make, create, fix, or do?

3. When it comes to working with your hands, what do you wish you could do? Why?
   - ❑ home repairs
   - ❑ fix cars
   - ❑ re-upholster furniture
   - ❑ construct models
   - ❑ paint pictures
   - ❑ build cabinets
   - ❑ plan interior decorating
   - ❑ work with power tools

Exploring the Text (20/35 minutes)

Selections from the life of Joseph

Read through each of the following passages, and discuss them using the questions below.

1. The prediction of Jesus' birth: Matthew 1:18–25
   - How do you think Joseph felt when he: heard that Mary was pregnant? Had his dream? Made Mary his wife?
   - In what ways does Joseph demonstrate that he is, indeed, a "righteous man" as he is called in verse 19?
   - What do you suppose Joseph wrote in his journal about the events leading up to Jesus' birth?

2. The birth of Jesus: Luke 2:1–20
   - Under what circumstances did the birth of Jesus take place?
   - What was Joseph's role in these events?
   - What might Joseph have written in his journal about Jesus' birth?

3. The presentation of Jesus at the Temple: Luke 2:21–40
   - What new information is given to Joseph about his son?
   - What might Joseph have written about his role and responsibility as a father to a child like Jesus?

4. The escape to Egypt: Matthew 2:13–23
   - How (and why) did Joseph and his family flee to Egypt? Return to Israel?
   - What might Joseph have written in his journal about the flight to Egypt, the consequences of Jesus' birth for the families in Bethlehem, living in Egypt as a foreigner, and his return to Israel?

5. Jesus at the age of twelve: Luke 2:41–52
   - Describe what the trip to Jerusalem must have been like for Jesus and his family. How did his family feel when they discovered that he was missing?
   - What might Joseph have written in his journal about his experience of Passover, his fright when Jesus was missing, and his wonder when he found him?

6. Jesus and his family: Matthew 13:53–58
   - How did the people of Nazareth respond to Jesus?
   - Why did they take such offense to him?
   - Joseph is probably dead at this point. What might his children have written about him in their eulogy?

Responding to the Text (20/30 minutes)

In your story:

1. Have you ever been involved in events that weren't what they seemed on the surface? Describe the situation.

2. What was Christmas like in your childhood home? How did you celebrate it?

3. What great events in your lifetime have changed the way things were? How did these events affect you?

4. Did your family move when you were a child? Where did you go? What was it like?

5. As a child, when (if ever) did you give your parents a scare like Jesus gave his parents?

6. Have you ever been upset with someone who you thought was "putting on airs"? Describe the situation. Has anyone responded to you like that? Why?

Journal Assignment (5 minutes)

In your journal, continue to explore the story of Joseph. Be attentive to the parallels between his story and your story. In your journal, explore further the incidents in your life that you recalled during the small group discussion. Be alert to new insights about your past that emerge through examining your experiences in light of Scripture. Use Joseph's story as a way to recall other incidents in your past. If you find it useful, write "the journal of Joseph" as a way of understanding his story in Scripture.

Background Notes

- **pledged to be married:** In the first century, betrothal was binding and could not be broken except by an act of divorce, even though the man and woman did not yet live together or have a sexual relationship. Mary and Joseph's betrothal was arranged by their parents (with their consent). It usually lasted a year and involved payment by the groom of a portion of the bridal price. Mary was most likely twelve to fourteen years of age, and Joseph was between eighteen and twenty.
- **adultery:** The laws of adultery applied to a betrothed couple. If Mary was pregnant (and not by Joseph), he was required to divorce her. (Under OT law, the penalty for infidelity was death, but by the first cen-

tury it was rarely applied.) If Mary had been divorced for infidelity (which resulted in the birth of a child), it would have been very difficult for her to find another husband. She would have been forced to live with her parents and would have had great trouble supporting herself.

- **dreams:** It was assumed by first-century people that God could (and did) speak through dreams. Thus Joseph treats his dreams as authentic messages from God—messages he must obey. Dreams are mentioned five times in the first two chapters of Matthew.

- **angel:** In the OT, angels often brought messages from God in dreams.

- **Jesus:** In Hebrew, the name "Jesus" means "God is salvation."

- **marriage:** Marriage involved a covenant (which included payment from one family to the other), a ceremony, and then the consummation of the marriage. Joseph completes the ceremony but waits until after the birth of Jesus to consummate the marriage.

- **house and line of David:** Jesus is related to David (and thus is the Son of David) through his father Joseph. Since Mary went with Joseph to register, she also was probably from the House of David.

- **purification:** After the birth of a son, the mother was required to offer a sacrifice for her purification forty days after the birth.

- **the child's father:** Joseph is the legal (though not the actual) father of Jesus.

- **Herod:** Herod was a brutal man: he killed his enemies, one of his wives, and some of his children. Ordering the deaths of these little boys was an extraordinarily vicious act.

- **Feast of the Passover:** By law, all adult Jewish males were required to participate in three feasts: Passover, Pentecost, and Tabernacles. This meant traveling to Jerusalem, usually accompanied by their families.

- **twelve:** This was one year before Jesus had his *bar mitzvah* and became an adult who was personally responsible for keeping the law of Moses.

- **caravans:** Communities traveled together to feasts like Passover, both for protection and for the fun and fellowship. It would have been easy for Jesus to get lost in the crowd and be off with his friends (which is what his parents probably assumed).

- **carpenter:** The Greek word refers to a craftsman who works in metal and stone as well as wood.

- **brothers/sisters:** Jesus' siblings, who were born to Mary and Joseph.

- **they took offense:** The people he grew up with couldn't forget Jesus' humble origins and working-class background. They couldn't imagine that he had power to heal, so they didn't ask (and were not healed).

---

[1] Progoff, p. 229.

[2] If you want to pursue dream interpretation further, consult a book like *Dreams and Spiritual Growth: A Christian Approach to Dreamwork* by Savary, Berne, and Williams (Paulist Press, 1984).

[3] This is the TTAQ dreamwork technique found in Savary, Berne, and Williams, pp. 22ff.

[4] *The Journals of Jim Elliot*, ed. by Elisabeth Elliot (Old Tappan, NJ: Fleming H. Revell Co., 1978).

Chapter Seven

Using Journals to Nurture Our Spiritual Lives

"To speak with God... how impossible. And yet... did not our fathers and mothers in the faith do so?"

For a Christian, journaling is a spiritual discipline. A journal enables us to remember, to probe, to question, and to understand our lives.

Journals also help us to nurture our spiritual lives. As we write, we wrestle with ideas, think theologically about life, and explore new concepts—all of which helps to form a Christian worldview. We seek to understand ourselves and offer our lives up to God. We wrestle with choices we face, and seek to know and do God's will. We commit ourselves to knowing God.

Journals aid us in the practice of other spiritual disciplines. For example:
- *Bible study:* In our journals we take notes on a passage, record our observations, write down our questions, and reflect on the passage.
- *Prayer:* In our journals we identify our requests, write out our prayers, copy other people's prayers as we learn to pray, and listen to what God is saying to us. [1]
- *Meditation:* In our journals we reflect on our lives and actions in the context of our Bible study and prayer.
- *Confession:* In our journals we tell God what we have done (which we ought not to have done) and what we have left undone (which we should have done).

Why are journals such a powerful force for spiritual change? There are several reasons. First, when we work in a journal, we put our thoughts, feelings, issues, and concerns into words on a page. The process of writing something down clarifies issues; it keeps us honest; it helps make us real. Second, journaling forces us to face ourselves and our unfolding lives. By working in a journal we are giving time to growth; we are actively working at it. Third, journals give us an ongoing record so that we know where we have come from, where we are, and where we are going. In knowing our past, we understand the present better and have a clearer reading of how our future will unfold. Finally, journals enable us to know our stories. As we work in our journals, we piece together the various elements of our particular story. In understanding the nature of our pilgrimage, we come to know who God wants us to be and what we are called to do. We discover questions which we need answers to; we see the choices we are called upon to make. In knowing our stories, we come to know God in our story. And that is a great gift.

PART ONE/Learning to Journal

Session Overview

Communication with God is at the heart of our spiritual life: talking and listening to him. A journal is an aid to both of these processes.

Two ways of journaling are suggested in this session. In the first, the Letter to God exercise, we use our journals to express to God what we're thinking, feeling, and wrestling with. In the second, the Prayer exercise, we use our journals to learn new ways to pray.

Telling Our Stories (15/20 minutes)

Experiences of God

A sense of God comes in different ways to different people: it is sometimes big and dramatic; at other times, small and quiet. Most of the time, we hardly notice.

1. When you were a child, in what ways were you aware of God? Explain.
   - ❏ in my prayers   ❏ in the Bible
   - ❏ in church   ❏ in nature
   - ❏ in certain experiences   ❏ in reading
   - ❏ in conversation   ❏ other: _____

2. What's been the most direct experience you've had of God?
   - ❏ a spine-tingling sense that God was present
   - ❏ joyous, overwhelming worship
   - ❏ a deep awareness of God's presence in nature
   - ❏ a mystical experience   ❏ an amazing answer to prayer
   - ❏ my conversion experience   ❏ nothing quite like any of this
   - ❏ an inner sense of his presence   ❏ other: _____

3. What was your conversion experience like? Or what's the nearest thing you've had to a conversion experience?

The Journal Method (5 minutes)

Just as we have tried Dialogue exercises with people and subjects (in chapter 4), so we can also dialogue with God. The process is the same: write two to four paragraphs that define the state of your relationship to God. In a meditative manner, begin a dialogue with God and record the unfolding conversation in your journal. Once you are finished, review and respond to the dialogue.

For some people, this is a good way to understand their relationship with God. However, many people find it difficult to do this exercise. It feels presumptuous to write down what we suppose God is saying. But the fact remains that we need to communicate with God. The following two exercises are alternate ways of doing the same thing: speaking to and listening to God.

Letter to God

The process is really quite simple. Write a letter to God. There is nothing more—or less—to the exercise. It helps, however, to have a perspective from which to write:

- **A note about everyday issues:** "Dear God, I'm sitting here worrying about Jerry again. He's a good kid, as you know, but he just can't get his act together. It's 11:00 a.m. and he still isn't home from the night he spent at Ben's house. So, another day of work is lost to partying. I'm so worried about him . . . ." In this way you define the issues that concern you and offer them to God.
- **A reflection on a period in your life:** "Dear God, I've spent the past few months working on my Kansas City phase of life. You know how troubled that time was. I'm really glad that it's past. Help me never again to have to go through something like that. So now I offer that period to you. Here is what I've made of it . . . ." In this way you offer to God your reflections on your past and, in prayer, seek to learn from it and leave it behind.
- **A meditation on an issue:** "Dear God, I don't understand why innocent children die. The tragedy in Rwanda haunts me. How could this happen? I know that you understand evil and death. You sent your own Son to suffer and die . . . ." In this way you examine your views on tough theological issues as you develop a Christian worldview.
- **A response to a challenge:** "Dear God, I know it's good for me to live next door to the Smiths, but frankly, they drive me crazy, what with their loud music and loud friends. I know I'm supposed to love them, but I don't. Please help me with this . . . ." In this way you work your way through a problem of Christian discipleship.

Prayer

When we think of talking to God, we automatically think of prayer. But prayer isn't one thing, it's many things. Our journal is a good place to learn new ways of prayer. You might want to experiment with the following three forms of prayer:

- **The Prayer of Examen:** This is a prayer used by Saint Ignatius, the founder of the Jesuits. It's a way of assessing our day before God. It has three parts to it. You can use your journal to answer each question. In the past twenty-four hours:
  1. Reflect on *what you have to be thankful for.* Let your prayer begin with joy and gratitude.

2. Reflect on *the ways in which you have met God.* Search through your day, pausing at the moments (mostly brief and incidental) in which God's Spirit was present.

3. Reflect on *the ways you have avoided or failed God.* In this atmosphere of thankfulness and awareness of God, offer up your sin and shortcoming, knowing that God forgives and heals.

- **The Prayer of Intercession:** In this prayer, we ask God (as he invites us to do) for what we—and others—need in life. In your journal write down your requests, based on the three petitions in the Lord's Prayer:

  1. *Give* (us this day our daily bread): In this way Jesus invites us to pray about matters of everyday living: food, clothing, illness, problems we face, relationships—all of the "mundane" issues of life can be brought to God.

  2. *Forgive* (us our debts): In this way we bring our sins, our burdens, our hurts, our shortcomings, our pain in relationships—every aspect of our relationships can be brought to God.

  3. *Deliver* (us from evil): In this way we offer to God the temptations we face: the desire for power, fame, money, acquisition, control—all of the many faces of evil can be brought to God.

- **The Prayer of Worship:** This is a prayer of response: adoration of and thanks to God for all of the wonders of life. We may need the help of others, since it's possible that we won't always have the words to express what's in our hearts. You might want to purchase a book such as *The Oxford Book of Prayer* [2] and search its pages until you find prayers that best express what you want to say. Copy these prayers into your journal. Pray them often until their language becomes yours. Write down your own prayers of wonder and worship. Make your journal a place of rich prayer. [3]

The Journal Exercise (15/30 minutes)

Preparation:
- Get out your journal. Find a comfortable spot in which to journal. Date your journal. Entitle the entry: Letter to God or Prayer (depending upon which exercise you want to do). File this in the Pilgrimage section of your journal.
- Go over the directions below that describe the journaling exercise.
- Do the focusing exercise, asking the Holy Spirit to lead you as you journal.
- Begin journaling, in silence, for the time allotted.

Process: choose one of the following exercises:
- *Letter to God:* Follow the instructions above, and write a letter to God. Instead of writing the letter, you may choose to do a dialogue with God, if you are comfortable with that. In either case, speak with God about issues that are significant to you.
- *Prayer:* Pick one of the prayer formats and use your journal to help you pray. Follow the instructions above.

Journal Sharing (20/30 minutes)

When you finish journaling, discuss your findings with the group.

1. Explore the process of journaling as you have experienced it in this course:
   - What aspects of journaling are the easiest for you? The most difficult? The most useful? Why?
   - What is your plan for continuing to journal once the group ends?
   - What is the most important thing you learned about how to journal?

2. Share your insights from the journal experience:
   - Which exercise did you do: the Letter to God or the Prayer exercise? Why did you select the one that you did?

   - For those who chose the Letter to God exercise:
     Which kind of letter did you write? Why?
     Read portions of your letter.
     What did you learn about your relationship to God from this exercise?

   - For those who chose the Prayer exercise:
     Which prayer did you explore?
     Read your prayer or share insights from the experience.
     What did you learn about prayer?

   - What new aspects of your story have you uncovered?

3. Discuss the next step for your small group. Now that this overview of journaling is almost completed, you are ready to start the second course in this series: *Spiritual Autobiography.* Your work in journals is the ideal preparation for starting and sharing a spiritual autobiography.

4. Pray together. Praise God for what you've learned about journaling as a spiritual discipline. Thank him for what you've learned about your pilgrimage.

Journaling Assignment (5 minutes)

During the next week:

- Read over all of the material in the chapter, including the excerpt from *Pensées*, the journal of Blaise Pascal.
- Explore your spiritual life. Identify experiences in which the life and presence of God was especially evident. Try new forms of prayer. Develop a new awareness of the spiritual side of your life.
- Ask God for help as you explore your spirituality.
- Discern what new insights you have into your unfolding story. What new things have you learned about who you are?
- Decide how you're going to continue to journal, now that this course is almost over.

Journal Readings

Pensées

Blaise Pascal was a genius. At age eleven, he wrote a paper about sound in vibrating objects. At sixteen, his article on Conic Sections won the respect of mathematicians in Paris. As an adult, he constructed a machine to do arithmetic calculations. He also developed the barometer and defined the general laws of pneumatics. In addition to his scientific accomplishments, he was a man of letters. His book, *The Provincial Letters*, was a major influence in French literature. Pascal was also a devout Christian. Toward the end of his life (he died at the age of thirty-nine), he started a book on evidences of religion. All he produced, however, were fragments. They were more like journal entries than book chapters. After his death, his friends published these as *Pensées*. The following excerpts show the use of a journal as a vehicle to clarify thoughts, to mull over ideas, and to develop theological understanding.

> *784: I consider Jesus Christ in all persons and in ourselves: Jesus Christ as a Father in His Father, Jesus Christ as a Brother in His Brethren, Jesus Christ as poor in the poor, Jesus Christ as rich in the rich, Jesus Christ as Doctor and Priest in priests, Jesus Christ as Sovereign in princes, etc. For by His glory He is all that is great, being God; and by His mortal life He is all that is poor and abject. Therefore He has taken this unhappy condition, so that He could be in all persons, and the model of all conditions.*

> *785: Jesus Christ is an obscurity (according to what the world calls obscurity), such that historians, writing only of important matters of states, have hardly noticed Him.*

> *791: What man ever had more renown? The whole Jewish people foretell Him before His coming. The Gentile people worship Him after His coming. The two peoples, Gentile and Jewish, regard Him as their centre.*

> *And yet what man enjoys this renown less? Of thirty-three years, He lives thirty without appearing. For three years He passes as an impostor; the priests and the chief people reject Him; His friends and His nearest relatives despise Him. Finally, He dies, betrayed by one of His own disciples, denied by another, and abandoned by all.*

> *What part, then, has He in this renown? Never had man so much renown; never had man more ignominy. All that renown has served only for us, to render us capable of recognizing Him; and He had none of it for Himself.*

> *796: Proofs of Jesus Christ—Jesus Christ said great things so simply, that it seems as though He had not thought them great; and yet so clearly that we easily see what He thought of them. This clearness, joined to this simplicity, is wonderful.* [4]

PART TWO/Bible Study

Session Overview

In our final Bible study, we will focus on David and the psalms he wrote. The Psalms are a type of journal. In them we can track the ups and downs in the life of David, the king loved by God. The Psalms are poetic cries to God. They are theological reflections: hymns of praise, cries of despair, longings for vengeance and vindication.

Look at incidents in the life of David and consider what his journal might have contained.

Telling Our Stories (15/20 minutes)

To be a warrior poet . . .

David was a man of action and a man of prayer. He was a king and a spiritual leader. He was active and he was contemplative. It is rare to find a person who expresses such contrasting sides. Most of us are one or the other.

1. Put an "✗" where you fit between the following contrasts:
   lover _____ fighter
   poet _____ priest
   contemplative _____ activist
   follower _____ leader
   feeler _____ doer

2. If you had to pick one of the ten characteristics above as the one that defines you best, which would it be? Why?

3. Which word or phrase best expresses the way you feel about the Psalms?
   ❐ inspiring   ❐ challenging
   ❐ wonderful   ❐ express my deepest longings
   ❐ mysterious   ❐ intimidating
   ❐ real   ❐ confusing

Exploring the Text (20/35 minutes)

Selections from the life of King David

Read through each of the following Psalms, and discuss them using the questions below. Each Psalm is a different kind of poem.

1. A Psalm of Lament: Psalm 3
   - What problem does David face, and what does he ask of God in light of it?
   - In what ways does God sustain David in this difficult time?
   - What might David have written in his journal about the revolt of his son, hiding in the wilderness, and learning to trust God?

2. A Psalm of Thanksgiving and Adoration: Psalm 8
   - What two things about God especially impress David?
   - How is the role and place of humanity described in this Psalm?
   - How might David have described that night standing on his balcony, the stars spread out above him and his kingdom spread out before him? What did he learn about God in that setting?

3. A Psalm of Wisdom: Psalm 15
   - How does David answer the question he asks in verse 1: who has access to God?
   - Describe the behavior that God requires of his people.
   - What might David have written in his journal about his struggles to live in this fashion?

4. A Psalm of Praise: Psalm 23
   - How does God treat his flock?
   - How does God treat his guests?
   - What might David have written in his journal about his experience of God as shepherd and host?

5. A Psalm of Penitence: Psalm 51
   - Identify the various words which describe what David seeks from God.
   - What picture of human nature is presented here?
   - How might David have written about the situation with Bathsheba and its aftermath?

6. A Royal Psalm: Psalm 110
   - What are the promises made to the king?
   - What might David's reflections have been about his role as king and priest?

Responding to the Text (20/30 minutes)

In your story:

1. Have you ever been in a terrible situation where you were powerless to do anything? What happened? What did you learn about God?

2. Describe a situation when you were overwhelmed with awe in the face of God's creation.

3. Which of these actions (in Psalm 15) is the easiest for you? Which is hardest?

4. What in your experience is like David's experience of God as the good shepherd and the gracious host?

5. How have you confronted your sin and the need for God's mercy?

6. In what ways have you known the royal rule of God in your life?

7. Compose your own psalm as a way of thanking God for what you have learned and experienced in this small group. Praise him for what he has done for you during this time. Ask him what the next step in your pilgrimage should be. Compose a prayer that you want to offer to God. End your final small group session by praying these psalms aloud.

Journal Assignment (5 minutes)

In your journal, continue to explore the Psalms of David. Be attentive to the parallels between his story and your story; his prayers and your prayers. In your journal, explore further the incidents in your life that you recalled during the small group discussion. Be alert to new insights about your past that emerge through examining your experiences in light of Scripture. Use the Psalms as a way to recall other incidents in your past, and as a way to enhance your worship of God. If you find it useful, write psalms as a way of responding to God.

Now you're on your own in your journal work. Continue to explore the past periods of your life. Recount your days in the Daily Log section of your journal. Pay attention to the various dimensions of your life. Use the various journal exercises (when necessary) to understand your story and hear God's word to you. *You will learn to journal as you journal.* Blessings on your venture in spiritual journaling.

Background Notes

- **The Psalms:** The Psalms are different from other books in the Bible in their literary format and theological intention. They were not written by one person or in one era. In fact, they are a collection of materials written over hundreds of years. Saint Athanasius said that "most of Scripture speaks to us, while the Psalms speak for us." They are prayers and praise addressed to God. They reveal our innermost longings and distress. The Psalms give voice to the human heart as it stands open before God.
- **A Psalm of David:** Superscriptions like this were not attached to the original Psalms and may have been added later by editors. Sometimes it is clear that they identify Psalms written by David. At other times, they indicate Psalms that are to be used in royal ceremonies, written about David or about one of the kings in his line.
- **Psalm 3:** A Psalm of lament in which David prayed for God's help. The superscription describes the background of this Psalm. David's son Absalom led a revolt against his father (see 2 Samuel 15ff.), and drove David into the wilderness.
- **Psalm 8:** A Psalm of thanksgiving and adoration to God (see the beginning and end of the Psalm). David is amazed that the God of all creation is aware of feeble human beings and has given us such an amazing place in his universe.
- **Psalm 15:** A Psalm of wisdom in which moral righteousness (a particular way of life)—not sacrifice or ritual—is described as the way to God.
- **Psalm 23:** A Psalm of praise to God. He is the good shepherd (who looks after his flock), and the good host (who prepares an abundant table for his guests). This is probably the best known of all the Psalms.
- **Psalm 51:** A Psalm of penitence in which David cried out to God for mercy for the awful thing he had done to Bathsheba and her husband (see 2 Samuel 11:1–12:25). In order to make Bathsheba his wife, David arranged for her husband's death.
- **Psalm 110:** A royal Psalm intended to be used at the coronation of a king. It is also a Psalm about the coming Messiah. It is widely quoted in the NT as referring to Christ (Matthew 22:43–45; Mark 12:36–37; Luke 20:42–44; Acts 2:34–36; Hebrews 1:13; 5:6–10; 7:11–28).
- **footstool:** Vanquished enemies were forced to sit at the feet of the conquering king.
- **priest:** Not only did David rule his people, he was also a religious leader for the nation.

---

[1] The process of reading the Bible reflectively is discussed in volume three in this series: *Lectio Divina: Understanding our Stories*, and methods of prayer are explored in volume four: *Meditative Prayer: Growing our Stories*.

[2] General editor: George Appleton, Oxford University Press, 1985.

[3] For more insight into the various forms of prayer, see *Prayer: Finding the Heart's True Home* by Richard Foster (HarperCollins, 1992).

[4] *Pensées* by Blaise Pascal, trans. by W. F. Trotter (New York: Random House; The Modern Library, 1941), pp. 275–279.

The Art of Leadership: Brief Reflections on How to Lead a Small Group

It's not difficult to be a small group leader. All you need is:
- The willingness to do so;
- The commitment to read through all of the materials prior to the session;
- The sensitivity to others that will allow you to guide the discussion without dominating it;
- The willingness to be used by God as a small group leader.

Here are some basic small group principles that will help you do your job:

- **Ask the questions:** Your role is to ask the questions. Let group members respond.

- **Guide the discussion:** Ask follow-up questions (or make comments) that draw others into the discussion and keep the discussion going. For example:
     "John, how would you answer the question?"
     "Anybody else have any insights into this question?"

- **Start and stop on time:** If you don't, people may be hesitant to come again since they never know when they will get home.

- **Stick to the time allotted to each section:** There is always more that can be said in response to any question. It's your job to make sure that the discussion keeps moving from question to question. Remember: it's better to cut off discussion when it's going well than to let it go on until it dies out.

- **Model answers to questions:** Whenever you ask a question to which everyone is expected to respond (for example, a "Telling Our Stories" question as opposed to a Bible study question), you, as leader, should be the first person to respond. In this way you model the right length—and appropriate level—of response.

- **Understand the intention of different kinds of questions:**
     Experience questions: The aim is to cause people to recall past experiences and share these memories with the group. There are no right or wrong answers to these questions. They facilitate the group process by getting people to share their stories and to think about the topic.
     Forced-choice questions: Certain questions will be followed by a series of suggested answers (with check-boxes). Generally, there is no "correct" answer. Options aid group members and guide their responses.

Analysis questions: These force the group to notice what the Bible text says and to explore it for meaning.

Application questions: These help the group make connections between the meaning of the text and their own lives.

Questions with multiple parts: Sometimes a question is asked and then various aspects of it are listed below. Ask the group members to answer each of the sub-questions. Their answers, taken together, will answer the initial question.

- **Introduce each section:** This may involve a brief overview of the focus, purpose, and topic of the new section and instructions on how to do the exercise.

  Guiding exercises: A major portion of your job will be introducing the journal exercise. This is the heart of the "Learning to Journal" experience. Details of how to lead each section will be found in the *Small Group Leader's Guide*, especially in the material on the first meeting.

  Make sure the group has heard and understood the information found in the "The Journal Method" section.

  "Journal Exercise": Explain the journaling process that will be followed. Make sure everyone understands what is expected.

  Guide the "Preparation" process and invite the group to begin journaling on their own.

  End the journaling process when time is up.

  Begin the discussion as outlined in the "Journal Sharing" exercise.

- **Comments:** Occasionally bring into the discussion some useful information from your own study. Keep your comments brief. Don't allow yourself to become the "expert" to whom everyone turns for "the right answer."

Small Group Leader's Guide
Notes on each Session

Introduction: Starting a Small Group for Spiritual Journaling

If you are the small group leader, it is important for you to read carefully the section entitled *The Art of Leadership: Brief Reflections on How to Lead a Small Group* (pp. 81–82). Prior to each session, go over the notes for that session (see below). These will focus on the specific materials in the session.

Recruiting members: All it takes to start a group is the willingness of one person to make some phone calls.

Preparing for the first session: Deliver a copy of this book to each potential group member. Ask them to read *The Art of Journaling* introduction (pp. 7–10). This describes what a journal is, how to create and use a journal, and why it's helpful to journal in a small group.

Number of meetings: You can meet for seven or fourteen weeks. If you choose the seven-week option, use Part One of each chapter ("Learning to Journal") each time you meet, and assign Part Two ("Bible Study") for optional homework. If you choose the fourteen-week option, simply follow the order of the book: Chapter One, Part One; Chapter One, Part Two; Chapter Two, Part One, etc.

Chapter One: Using Journals Down Through History

The first meeting

The special character of session one: The first session is very important. People who attend will be deciding whether they want to be a part of the group. So your aim as small group leader is to:
- Create excitement about this small group (so each person will want to continue);
- Give people an overview of the series (so they know where they are headed);
- Begin to build relationships (so that a sense of community starts to develop);
- Encourage people to commit to the small group (so everyone will return next week, and perhaps bring a friend!).

Pot luck: A good way to start a small group is to share a meal before the first session. Eating draws people together and breaks down barriers between them. The aim of the meal is to get to know one another. Structure the meal in a way that a lot of conversation takes place.
Following the meal, be sure to do the first session in its totality (don't talk about what you're going to do when the group starts). Your aim is to give everyone the experience of being a part of this small group.

Introduction to the Series

Welcome: Greet people and let them know you're glad that they've come, and that you look forward to being with them for the next seven (or fourteen) weeks.
Prayer: Pray briefly, thanking God for this group and asking him to guide your deliberations and sharing today. Ask God to help you all learn how to use a journal as an aid for spiritual growth.

Group Process: Describe how the small group will function and what it will study. Discuss, specifically:
- **Series Theme:** The aim is to learn how to use a journal as a tool for spiritual growth.
- **Group Experience:** Explain that Part One of each chapter begins with a brief time of sharing where the topic is introduced through experiences that group members have had ("Telling our Stories"). Then you will investigate a particular method of journaling ("The Journal Method") and use that method during a time of individual journaling ("The Journal Exercise"). In the "Journal Sharing" time, you will discuss your experiences together, both in terms of process (what you learned about journaling) and outcome (what you learned about yourself).

  In the Part Two of each chapter, the group explores a series of passages which tell the story of someone in the Bible. After an opening exercise ("Telling Our Stories"), the texts are read and discussed from the vantage point of what that person might have written in a journal about each event or experience ("Exploring the Text"). Then members will look for parallels between that person's story and their own ("Responding to the Text").

- **Group Details:** Describe where you will meet, when, and how long each session will last.
- **Group Aims:** Share the aims of the group: that each person's spiritual growth will be enhanced, and that each will have discerned more clearly the story of his or her spiritual pilgrimage.

Part One: Learning to Journal

Telling Our Stories
- Give the group a minute to look over the questions.
- Begin the sharing. As leader, you should be the first one to answer each question. (Note, however, that this is true only for relational questions. Generally you ask questions and let the group respond.) Go around the group and give each person the chance to respond to the first question. Do the same for each question until time is up for the exercise.

  Question 1: Listen carefully to the various reasons that drew people to the group. This is the implicit agenda. These are the needs, hopes, and issues which the group needs to deal with.

  Question 2: There are two aims here: to help people remember their experiences of journaling, and to broaden their view of what a journal is. "Journal," as used here, means "a personal record of our past—oral or written."

The Journal Method
You will have to decide how to communicate the information in this section. This is the "theory" that underlies the "Journal Exercise." You don't want to take a lot of time to share this material, but it is vital information that the group needs in order to understand the exercise that follows. Options for sharing include:
- *Individual reading:* Give the group a few minutes to read the material on their own.
- *Leader presentation:* Read this material aloud while people follow along in their books, or summarize the section briefly.
- *Homework:* Ask the group to prepare for each session by reading the material in this section before you meet.

The Journal Exercise (with the Focusing Exercise)

- Go over the instructions. Make sure each person understands the nature of the exercise well enough to work effectively during the silent journaling period.
- Explain the nature of the focusing exercise. Since you will use this exercise to begin each period of journaling, take time to explain it adequately.
- *Preparation:* The aim is for people to relax and focus on the subject at hand. Sometimes it takes a while for us to set aside other concerns ("Will I enjoy this group?" "How am I going to solve that problem at work?" etc.).
- *Focusing Exercise:* There are two parts to this—relaxation and prayer.
  1. Relaxation: Ask people to find a comfortable place to sit. Make sure everyone has pen and paper as well as something to write on. Usually it works best to sit in a chair, both feet on the floor. Then:

  Have people close their eyes and start to relax.

  Ask them to relax the muscles first in their legs, then their stomachs, then their arms, and then their throats. Relaxation of the throat is especially important, since many people are tense here.

  Next, ask people to slow down their breathing; to inhale and exhale slowly several times.

  Then, with their eyes still closed, pray.

  2. Prayer:

  Pray that God the Holy Spirit will guide the exercise, leading people to insights and memories that are important for them.

  Pray that God will protect each person from evil so that their reflections will direct them to God, and that what they experience will be from him.

  Pray that the discussion which follows the journaling will bring insight, clarity, and fellowship.

The relaxation and prayer should take no more than a few minutes. The rest of the "Journal Exercise" is then spent in silence. Each person should work in his or her journal.

Journal Sharing

There are three parts to this:

- **In the first part,** the sharing focuses on the journaling process. It is important, especially in the first two or three sessions, to talk about method. Some people find journaling to be very easy. But others have difficulty "getting it right." Talking about doing the exercise is a way for each person to learn more about the art of journaling. You may want to reduce or even eliminate this part in later sessions in order to have more time for personal sharing.
- **In the second part,** you come to the heart of journal sharing: telling your stories to one another, based on what you have discovered as a result of journaling. When the journaling goes well, people will be eager to share their findings. In fact, this will be your major problem as group leader: guiding the discussion so that everyone has time to share and no one dominates.
- **In the final part** of this session, commit your discussion to God in prayer. Allow each person to share one request. Then pray together. There are various ways to do this:

  Free prayer: Ask people to pray as they feel led. As leader, keep track of each person's request so that when you conclude in prayer, you can remember the requests which haven't been prayer for yet.

Circle prayer: Ask each person to pray for the person on his or her right. This will only work with a group which is comfortable with spontaneous prayer.

Written prayer: After sharing requests, allow two minutes for everyone to compose a short prayer. This is useful for groups which are learning to pray aloud.

Conversational prayer: Invite members to pray sentence prayers, to pray more than once, and to pray in such a way as to build on each other's prayers. Make your prayer a group conversation with God.

Leader prayer: If time is short, you may want to close the session with prayer. Or you may ask someone else to do so (but be sure he or she is comfortable with praying aloud).

When you've decided on a format which is appropriate for your group, describe how you will pray together. Later on, you may want to change formats.

Journaling Assignment
Use the remaining time to go over the weekly assignment:

- *Reinforce* the fact that people will learn to journal by journaling. It is important to spend some time journaling between group sessions.
- *Discuss* the challenge to find time to journal. Ask a few people to share when they journal. Urge people to decide on specific times when they can journal each week.
- *Point out* that their assignment is to continue to explore the Present Period as a way of identifying the elements of their current life.
- *Make it clear* that each person will be given two minutes to share from his or her journal at the start of the next session (if you choose this option).

Concluding Issues
- *Group Invitation:* If your first session is a "trial meeting," invite everyone to return next week. If you have room in the group (i.e., there are less than twelve people), encourage members to invite their friends. After week two, new people cannot join the group, since each time a new person comes it is necessary to rebuild the sense of community. Ask people to turn to page 6 and read the Small Group Covenant. Explain that they will be asked to agree to these guidelines next week if they decide to continue with the group.

Part Two: Bible Study

Study Options
There are various ways to conduct this session:

- *Option one:* Proceed as a normal small group Bible study. Introduce the session briefly (welcome people, pray, give an overview). Do the history-giving exercise ("Telling Our Stories"). Work through the texts using the questions ("Exploring the Text") and conclude with application ("Responding to the Text").
- *Option two:* Do this as a journaling exercise. There are two ways to do this:
    Ask each person to silently study each of the passages. Have them scan the texts to find the answers to the questions, and then write the response to the final question for each text.
    Assign one or two passages to each person. This will give more time for more detailed study. Leave time for discussion so that the whole group gets a look at each passage.

This journaling exercise is a way of paraphrasing, where a person restates the passage from another perspective. It's an enjoyable activity that brings out the creativity in people. Conclude by using the "Responding to the Text" questions with the whole group.

Introduction to the Session

The second part of each chapter is a Bible study. Since this is a different format from last week, take adequate time to go over how the small group will work through this material.

Welcome: Greet people and let them know you're happy that they've returned.
Prayer: Pray briefly, thanking God for this group and asking him to guide your deliberations and sharing today as you examine the life of Barnabas.
Group Process: Describe the Bible study process. You will begin with a history-giving exercise as you did in the first session (and will do in each session). This is followed by examination of various texts which relate to a particular person in the Bible. This week Barnabas is the focus of study. After your study, you will then make connections between Barnabas' life and each member's life.
Group Aims: The aim of the Bible study is to creatively reflect on what the journal of a person from the Bible might look like. Other people's stories often spark insights into our own.

Telling Our Stories

- Give the group a minute to read the questions and decide on answers.
- As leader, you should be the first one to answer each question. Go around the group and give each person a chance to respond.

Exploring the Text

How you present the text depends on which option you have chosen for this exercise. If you want the entire group to study each of the texts, ask someone ahead of time to read one or two of them aloud. The rest may be read in silence—there is not enough time to read all of the texts aloud.

- Since you'll often read long passages, you cannot study any one of them in depth. You need to skim the material. The "Exploring the Text" questions will help focus your attention. Mastering the art of skimming is important in Bible study. Often we focus so intensely on certain verses that we miss the flow of the whole passage. The Bible study in this book scans a lot of material rather than analyzes anything in great detail. Make sure the group understands this—otherwise some people may be frustrated (since their Bible study experience has been to focus on a few verses).
- Once each text is read, discuss it before moving to the next passage. Watch the time. Each passage is so rich that you could spend your time on only one, and not look at the others. The aim is to do a quick survey of the life of Barnabas.
- The initial questions concern the details of the text. The final question in each set focuses on Barnabas' response to the situation. This is the key question.
- The "Background Notes" will give some historical details that deepen the group's understanding of the text. There may not be enough time to do anything more than glance at these notes. You may wish to draw attention to certain notes that give important information.

- Questions that ask you to "describe" an incident are calling for a paraphrase of it. In this way, the group grasps the essence of the passage.
- You may not have time to get through each passage. Be sure to skim all the passages, even if you don't discuss each of them.

Responding to the Text
The aim in this section is to use Barnabas' experience to reflect on the lives of the group members. In these questions you will be looking for parallels, contrasts, and similarities. The hope is that by reflecting on Barnabas' life, the members' lives will be clarified and their past understood in a new way.
- There are two ways of doing this exercise:
  1. Use the questions in this section as the basis for your discussion; or
  2. Use the questions as the basis for silent journaling. In this case, end the session by asking each person to take one minute to share the key insight that he or she got from Barnabas' life.
- As you can see, there is one set of "Response" questions for each text. It may be easier to discuss each text and immediately ask the Responding to the Text" questions before going on to the next text. In that case, you might want to select some of the six texts to concentrate on, and ask people to examine the others as part of their homework.

Concluding Issues
- *Group Covenant:* In the second session, it is important to discuss the ground rules for the group (see p. 6). Ask the group to turn to the section entitled: *The Study Guide at a Glance.* Give the group a few minutes to look over the Small Group Covenant. Discuss the ground rules. Make sure everyone is comfortable with them. End by going around the group and giving everyone an opportunity to agree to the final group covenant.
- *Group Homework:* It is important to continue journaling during the week. Continue to explore the story of Barnabas and work on the journal, reflecting on what you learn from his life.
- *Group Prayer:* End with a time of prayer. (Choose from the list of prayer options on pp. 85–86.)

Chapter Two: Using Journals to Cope with Our Present

The basic outline for how to proceed in each of the two small group sessions in this chapter is given in the notes for Chapter One. Refresh your memory for how the group works by going over these notes first and then looking at the specific details for this chapter.

Part One: Learning to Journal

Telling Our Stories
This week you have an option. Since your group has been journaling during the week, you may wish to begin by allowing each person to share briefly one important insight he or she has gained as a result of their work. The advantage of beginning this way is to encourage people to journal during the week. Also, the insights will be fresh and pertinent. This is a great way for group members to get to know one another quickly. If you choose this option:

- Divide the time available for this exercise (15–20 minutes) by the number of people in the group. This defines the maximum amount of time each person can share. For example: if you have 20 minutes available, in a group of 10 people each person would be able to share for two minutes.
- As leader, you should begin the sharing. Then go around the circle and let each person share. Watch the time and gently reign in group members who take too long to share.
- Allow anyone to say "Pass" when it is his or her turn if that person does not wish to share.

You may choose, however, to use the "Life is such a rush" exercise. Or you might combine both options, allowing time for brief sharing from journals and ending with one of the questions from the exercise.

- Since the focus of this journaling session is on a Daily Log, the sharing exercise looks at how we organize our days, with stress on the pressures we face in our daily routines.

The Journal Method

Read or summarize the text to communicate the vital information in this section. It is crucial that group members understand the concept of a Daily Log in order for them to do the journal exercise successfully.

The Journal Exercise

Go over the instructions with the group. Make sure each person understands the exercise well enough to work effectively during the silent journaling period.

- Start the focusing exercise, and help people to relax. Pray for God's guidance and protection.
- Invite the group to journal in silence and to follow the instructions in the text.

Journal Sharing

Discuss both the process of journaling (what was learned about this journal method) and the results of journaling (new insights into the lives of group members).

- End with a time of focused prayer about the issues that emerged during the sharing.

Journaling Assignment

Use the final few minutes to go over the weekly assignment.

Concluding Issues

If this is your second meeting, be sure to go over the Small Group Covenant. See instructions under "Concluding Issues" at the end of the Leader's Notes for Chapter One, Part Two (page 88).

Part Two: Bible Study

Telling Our Stories

The focus of the questions is on zeal (which was a key characteristic of Paul). This particular set of questions illustrates how texts from Scripture help us to understand our own stories. As we seek to understand Paul's zeal, we also try to understand the role zeal has (or has not) played in our lives. In this way we may note something about our stories that we were not aware of.

Exploring the Text

Work on the various passages by using the small group method you decided on in your first Bible study session.

- Remember that you want a composite picture of Paul. Do not get bogged down with any single passage. It will take some discipline to keep the group moving.
- Remember that your primary aim is to imagine what Paul might have written in his journal at various key points in his life.

Responding to the Text

The goal of your exploration of key incidents in Paul's life is insight into your own stories. Use the questions in this section to identify and discuss what you discover.

Concluding Issues

- Go over the homework assignment.
- Pray together about the issues which were raised in your conversation.

Chapter Three: Using Journals to Recover Our Past

Part One: Learning to Journal

Telling Our Stories

The focus of the journal exercise is on recovering our past. It will help the group "remember" some of the good times that happened "back then."

- The questions here concentrate on seeing life as a series of time frames, each with its own distinctive character.

Journal Exercise

The numbers are important—they divide life into the right amount of periods. With fewer than eight periods, you will explore time frames that are too long; with more than twelve, the time frames are too short.

Journal Sharing

- In part one, ask about the ease or difficulty in identifying eight to twelve hinge events. For some people, such a list comes easily and spontaneously; for others, it's a much more difficult exercise. Assure people that whatever list they came up with will suffice as a way to define the structure of their past.
- Begin the second part by asking two or three people to read their list of hinge events. Then you might ask others to identify some of the hinge-events they found. Ask which periods captured their attention and why.
- By now you realize how important the prayer time is. Prayer which is based on deep personal insight—in the context of a group of like-minded people—is a powerful experience. Be sure to leave plenty of time for prayer. You will probably find that the group needs more and more time for prayer after each session.

Part Two: Bible Study

Telling our Stories

The focus of the questions is on courtship. These questions may be tricky to ask in some groups since: a) not everyone is married, b) not everyone wants to be married, or c) some people wonder about their marriage! But since courtship and marriage are such crucial topics in our unfolding stories, plunge right in and explore the topic in a way which is appropriate to your group. Remember:

- Keep it light. The opening exercise isn't meant to be heavy. Make this exercise fun.
- Adapt the questions. The instructions in this exercise ask people to apply the questions to their own circumstances. Help people to do this. For those who aren't married, shift the questions to the process of finding friends.

Exploring the Text

In this session, you will quickly scan the Book of Ruth. Since you want an overview of Ruth's life (and not a detailed analysis of it), watch the time carefully and guide the group.

- Remember the intention of the questions in this section: they help group members notice what is in the text (the process of observation), and they encourage group members to reflect on the meaning of the text (the process of interpretation). These are the first two steps in the inductive Bible study process.

Responding to the Text

In this section, you connect the meaning of the text to the life of each group member (the process of application). This is the final step in the inductive Bible study process.

- Remember that some application questions work with some people; others won't. Don't push applications that are inappropriate.

Chapter Four: Using Journals to Interact with Our Histories

Part One: Learning to Journal

Telling Our Stories

The focus in the journal exercise is on interacting with people through the process of journal dialogue. This exercise encourages people to think about friendship.

- It will be interesting to compare what people consider the key characteristic of a good friend to be. This list could be used to critique what kinds of friends we are. Which characteristic describes how we relate as a friend to others?

The Journal Method

Journal dialogues will be unfamiliar to some people and downright strange to others. Encourage people to suspend their doubts until they try it. The experience itself is usually enough to convince most people of the value of journal dialogue. For those who remain unconvinced, there is no need for them to pursue this method any further. There are many other ways for them to work in their journals.

The Journal Exercise
Since this is a multi-part exercise, be sure to allow plenty of time.
- One of the instructions is to read the journal dialogue aloud when it is complete. This is not possible when journaling in a group, so ask people to read it silently. Later on, when they are alone, people can read their entries aloud.

Journal Sharing
Be sure to discuss the process of journaling, since this is a new kind of exercise. Some people may have had difficulty doing it, so the group's help will be useful.

Part Two: Bible Study

Telling Our Stories
The first two questions probe energetic people and energetic activity. The project or mission doesn't have to be something huge: teaching Vacation Bible School, putting together a drama group, reading the works of Hemingway one summer—all of these qualify as "enthusiastic responses." What you want people to recall is what it's like when they are motivated and energized.
- *Question 3:* Although the question is phrased "the biggest 'goof,' " any "goof" will do.

Responding to the Text
Most people do not come to understand Jesus in a flash. Most grow into that understanding. However, many people can recall certain incidents—a sermon, a conversation, a book—in which they received new insights about Jesus. Remember that there may be some in your group who do not understand who Jesus is, or have not committed their lives to him. Give space to those who are still on a pilgrimage when it comes to meeting and understanding Jesus.
- *Question 3:* This is not an easy question to answer. No one likes to remember betrayals. Still, we are all guilty of such acts. It may be as innocent and understandable as bad-mouthing a friend in high school, or it may be as agonizing as an unfaithful spouse. The depth of sharing will be determined by the level of trust that has been generated in the group. Note that the question can be answered in two ways: sharing about our betrayals or about being betrayed.

Chapter Five: Using Journals to Realize Our Future

Part One: Learning to Journal

Telling Our Stories
What we actually become is something different from our dreams in childhood and high school. It is a mix of training, circumstances, networking, social needs, and economics. Still, sometimes you will find important paths for the future buried in past plans. Maybe that little boy who wanted to be a fireman will join the auxiliary police, become an EMT and work on an ambulance two nights a week, or even join a volunteer fire department—thus fulfilling the desire to help others in emergencies.

The Journal Method

Three journal methods are touched upon here. They are variations on a single theme, however: understanding future directions. The main exercise focuses on crossroads experiences and discerning whether the road not taken still needs to be explored. A variation on that exercise suggests that if a person is at a crossroads right now, he or she should try to imagine where various paths might take them. The remaining exercise ("Patterns") is described only briefly. It is a natural extension of the work that's been done with different periods. Suggest that the group try the "Patterns" exercise during the week.

The Journal Exercise and Sharing

By now you have established a regular pattern with the group. Continue with what you've been doing.

Part Two: Bible Study

Telling our Stories

This is a different kind of exercise. It involves determining (by a somewhat unscientific method) which of two personality types each person tends to be. The reason for doing this is that the two sisters in the Bible study reflect opposite personalities. With this background information, their story is better understood.

- Personality types exist on a scale. If people check all the answers in one column, they are an intense example of that personality type. If people check two answers in one column and three in the other, they are borderline.
- *Note:* In some circumstances it is important to be well-organized, while in other circumstances this tendency drives people crazy. "Your strength is your weakness," as someone once said.

Responding to the Text

- *Questions 2 and 3:* These are not easy issues to deal with. But by this time, the group should be close enough so that it's safe to discuss painful subjects. In fact, a small group can help us work through grief and pain even though it is long after the fact (but not dealt with at the time).

Chapter Six: Exploring Our Inner World

Part One: Learning to Journal

Telling Our Stories

The questions will help group members to explore their creative side. Many of us don't view ourselves as creative. Hence it is important to discover the ways in which we are.

The Journal Exercise and Sharing

Either exercise will yield useful insights.

Part Two: Bible Study

Telling our Stories
This is a follow-up to the previous journal exercise in which creativity was discussed and explored.

Responding to the Text
- *Question 1:* God is at work in the world to bring about events long foretold. Often in our lives, things take place that appear to be one thing but are really another. For example, it seems cruel that the kids have displaced their father as head of the family business, but only they know that Dad had been fiddling with the books and they were trying to get the business back on a sound footing.
- *Question 2:* Christmas can be a time of great joy or great woe. Family dynamics often come out at this particular holiday. The first Christmas was a mixed blessing for Mary and Joseph. What do people learn about themselves and their family dynamics from Christmas?
- *Question 3:* In almost every life, events happen that shift the world around us. The coming of Jesus changed the history of the world. In our lives, there are various national or international events that alter how we view the world or how we live life. Things like wars, economic ups and downs, elections, and natural disasters have this effect.

Chapter Seven: Using Journals to Nurture Our Spiritual Lives

Part One: Learning to Journal

Telling our Stories
To address the question of spiritual life, you must begin with each person's experience of and relationship to God. These questions facilitate this sort of conversation.
- *Question 3:* An experience of God is one thing; responding to God is another. Often the experience of God's presence causes us to commit our lives to God. Conversion experiences (turning to God in repentance and faith in Jesus) happen in a variety of ways. The question is purposely vague. It does not seek to define a conversion experience. It is really asking for a recollection of events in life when a person shifts direction because of conviction and because God intervenes in some way. This can happen suddenly (as it did to Paul) or gradually (as it did to the twelve apostles). While conversion to Christianity is a singular event, we experience many kinds of God-directed conversions over the course of our lives: both large and small shifts that move us in a God-ward direction. Let group members recall their conversions. If you run out of time, suggest that people use their journals to recall "conversions" they have had.

The Journal Exercise
Simply follow the patterns that have been established.

Journal Sharing

Notice that the first set of questions in this final chapter focus on the experience of learning to journal together over these past few weeks, and not on this one journaling exercise alone. Use this time to sum up what you have all learned about journaling.

It will be up to you to lead the discussion on the next step for the group. Do this in your final session (which will be this session for those groups doing only the journaling exercise, or next session for those groups also doing the Bible study). There are various options:

- Spiritual Autobiography: The second book in this series is entitled: *Spiritual Autobiography: Sharing Our Story.* It is the next logical step after spending time together and learning how to journal. During your time in this book, you have heard pieces of each other's story. In the next small group series, you will have the chance to hear the whole story. Each person has a small group session to himself or herself to share their spiritual autobiography, based on the guidelines in the book.
- Journaling Group: Continue to journal together. Rather than exploring new aspects of journaling, use the time to do three things:
    Begin by allowing each person to read a portion from his or her journal.
    Spend an extended time, in silence, journaling together.
    End by discussing new insights which were gleaned from the journaling time, and then pray for each other.
- Bible Study: Start a Bible study group together in which you explore a book or topic in the Bible. For example, you might want to consider the LEARNING TO LOVE series of Bible studies (also published by Pilgrimage and NavPress).

Part Two: Bible Study

Telling Our Stories

These questions focus on the characteristics of David (and us), and on how we relate in different ways to the Psalms at different times in our lives.

Exploring the Text

- *Question 1:* David is in a tight situation. In hiding, and anguished over the betrayal of his son and the revolt of his people, he cries out to God to protect him and to destroy his enemies. In the Psalms of lament one often finds prayers of destruction.

Responding to the Text

Note: Make sure you save time for question 7, even if you have to skip over some of the earlier questions.

- *Question 4:* The aim of this question is to help people identify times when they felt cared for, safe, and honored. Such times teach us how God loves us and cares for us all the time.
- *Question 5:* We all need mercy. Whether members answer this question in general terms or with their personal experience, explore this aspect of life.
- *Question 7:* Composing and praying psalms is a fine way to end the group time. Also, be sure to complete your plans for the next step for your small group. Plan the date and time for the next session; decide on a meeting place; order the small group books; etc.

A Select Bibliography

Books about Journaling

Kelsey, Morton T. *Adventure Inward: Christian Growth through Personal Journal Writing*. Minneapolis, MN: Augsburg Publishing House, 1980.

Klug, Ronald. *How to Keep a Spiritual Journal*. Nashville, TN: Thomas Nelson Publishers, 1982.

Progoff, Ira. *At a Journal Workshop: The basic text and guide for using the Intensive Journal*. New York: Dialogue House Library, 1975.

Santa-Maria, Maria L. *Growth Through Meditation and Journal Writing: A Jungian Perspective on Christian Spirituality*. New York: Paulist Press, 1983.

Simons, George F. *Keeping Your Personal Journal*. New York: Paulist Press, 1978.

Solly, Richard, and Roseann Lloyd. *Journey Notes: Writing for Recovery and Spiritual Growth*. San Francisco: Harper & Row, Publishers, 1989.

Examples of Journals

There are, by one count, at least 9,000 journals and diaries in print. Some examples follow:

Elliot, Jim. *The Journals of Jim Elliot*. Ed. by Elisabeth Elliot. Old Tappan, NJ: Revell, 1978.

Frank, Anne. *Diary of Anne Frank*. Garden City, NY: Doubleday, 1967.

Hammarskjöld, Dag. *Markings*. Trans. by W. H. Auden & Leif Sjoberg. London: Faber and Faber, 1964.

Kierkegaard, Søren. *The Journals of Søren Kierkegaard*. Trans. by Alexander Dru. London: Collins, Fontana Books, 1958.

Livingstone, David. *Livingstone's Private Journals (1851–1853)*. Ed. by I Schapera. Berkeley, CA: University of California Press, 1960.

Pascal, Blaise. *Pensées*. Trans. by W. F. Trotter. New York: The Modern Library, Random House, 1941.

Saint Augustine. *Confessions*. Trans. by Henry Chadwick. Oxford: Oxford University Press, 1992.

Thielicke, Helmut. *African Diary: My Search for Understanding*. Waco, TX: Word, 1974.

Wesley, John. *The Journals of John Wesley: A Selection*. Ed. by Elisabeth Jay. Oxford: Oxford University Press, 1987.